Top Dogs
Making it to
Westminster

✠✠✠

Deborah Wood

Hungry Minds™

New York, NY • Cleveland, OH • Indianapolis, IN

Howell Book House
Hungry Minds, Inc.
909 Third Avenue
New York, NY 10022

Howell Book House is a registered trademark of Hungry Minds, Inc.

For general information on Hungry Minds books in the U.S., please call our Consumer Customer Service department at 800-762-2974. For reseller information, including discounts and premium sales, please call our Reseller Customer Service department at 800-434-3422.

LOC: 2001093379

ISBN: 076456367X

Manufactured in United States of America

10 9 8 7 6 5 4 3 2 1

Cover design by Edwin Kuo
Cover photo by Meredith Parmelee/Tony Stone Images

Contents

Contents

Dedication

··

To America's 60 million dogs: purebred and mixed breed,
show dogs, couch potatoes, working dogs, and dogs desperately
waiting in shelters for their forever families to find them.
Every dog deserves to be Best in Show in someone's heart.

Acknowledgments

....

I don't know why anyone thinks that writing is a lonely profession. For me, it's always full of help and collaboration from all kinds of wonderful people. This book is no exception.

I conducted hundreds of hours of interviews and was given volumes of information by dozens of knowledgeable people. If I individually thanked all the people who gave their time, talent, and information helping me with this book, the acknowledgments would be as long as the text. I hope they know when they see their stories in this book that I am grateful to them beyond words. Their stories gave this book life.

I want to express my special appreciation to Dorothy Macdonald, Susan Hamil, Marilu Hansen, Gilbert Kahn, and Scott Sommer who told me the details of life in the Best in Show ring. Because of their candid, often funny, insights, I was able to write a book about America's top dogs from the vantage point of a front-row seat.

Howell Book House has been an enthusiastic and supportive partner in this great adventure. Thank you, Kathy Nebenhaus, for believing in this book and committing the resources to make it the best it can be; in an era of indifferent publishers, it's such a joy to have one work so hard to make a book succeed. Kira Sexton has been a kind, brainy, and caring editor who helped me through the marathon of writing this book. Scott Prentzas thought up the idea for this book, and Dominique De Vito had the faith in me to ask me to write the story. I feel honored and humbled to have worked with such wonderful people, and to have been entrusted with this grand project.

My fellow dog writers have been of great help and inspiration—giving me ideas, leads, and contacts. Thanks to Ranny Green for getting me started on this book—and on my writing career. Janine Adams, Andrea Arden, Sue Jeffries, and Chris Walkowicz went out of their way to help me—and gave me important contacts that made this book possible. The Dog Writers Association of America not only has fabulous writers in its ranks—it has the kindest, most supportive people imaginable.

The people in the Portland, Oregon, dog-show world opened doors based on their personal relationships. Special thanks are certainly due to Kathy Corbett and Patti Strand, who have helped me so much through the years, and helped enormously on this book.

My writing critique group, led by Myrla Magness, made sure that this manuscript made sense to those who don't spend every waking hour thinking about dogs.

I have a whole group of dog friends who helped with my dogs and my ability to function during the marathon of writing this book. Leah Atwood, Jill Miller, Robin Thompson, Ellie Wyckoff—thank you for being my friends, listening to the stories, and keeping one foot moving past the other when I was totally exhausted. Thank you also, Dale DeRoest and Tobie Hannah, for your helpful ideas, and for being friends as well as family.

No acknowledgment would be complete without thanking the creatures who bring me incredible joy every day of my life—my three Papillon dogs and my shelter kitty. Thank you, my sweet muses: Goldie (Wunsum Bit Lit Golden Girl CD CGC), Radar (U-CDX Aranon Music Maestro Please CDX HIC CGC), Pogo the puppy (La Ren I Go By Pogo), and the patient Mews. The best part of being a writer is spending every day with you.

Chapter 1

Glory at The Garden

It's down to seven dogs.

These dogs—along with the professional handlers who have preened and primped them, trained and prayed over them—stand in the ring with judge Dorothy Macdonald. She alone will pick the dog who will go Best in Show at the 2001 Westminster Kennel Club Dog Show. The names of six of the dogs will, in time, be lost in obscurity. The one who wins will be remembered in the annals of dogdom for the next hundred years.

Ten million television viewers are watching the show as it is broadcast live. Fifteen thousand screaming spectators in Madison Square Garden are cheering on their favorites.

The dogs are gaited around the ring in a circle, and the crowd screams. Most of the cheers go for the Bloodhound. People in the know agree that the crowd won't sway Dorothy Macdonald. She also won't be influenced by the names of the owners and backers of these show dogs. This longtime dog woman has a reputation for looking for movement, soundness, and quality. She doesn't care diddly-squat whose money is backing these dogs.

Make no mistake about it: A lot of money has been invested. In the past year alone, more than $1 million has been spent collectively on the seven dogs in this ring—paying for professional handlers, groomers, jet travel, and advertising in dog-show magazines. All of it for this one moment. All of it with the hope of having this judge point to their dog as Best in Show.

Winning brings with it no monetary award—just a silver bowl, as precious in the dog fancy as the chalice that was the Holy Grail.

Winning at Westminster is like no other honor in dogdom. The dog who wins the Westminster Kennel Club becomes a household name. He—or she—becomes the canine equivalent of Secretariat or Mario Andretti.

Dorothy Macdonald walks over to the judge's table. She calmly writes down a number and the breed of the winner, then takes the Best in Show purple-and-gold ribbon and stands in front of the seven dogs.

But to understand what it means when Macdonald names the winning dog, you need to take a step back in time.

Chapter 2

A Star Is Born

··

It was a long trip from Laguna Beach in Southern California to the ranch in the middle of Texas, but Susan LaCroix Hamil had a date with destiny. She carefully followed the directions: Drive the rental van from the Dallas/Fort Worth airport to Waco and turn right; keep driving through the empty Texas ranching country, and you'll come to a Dairy Queen. That's where she'd meet Elaine Woodson, to follow Elaine out to the ranch.

Susan's excitement mounted as she drove up to the sprawling Texas ranch. This was a red letter day—the day she was going to pick out her next show puppy. A dog who just might have a shot at winning the Westminster Kennel Club Dog Show.

Susan didn't travel a thousand miles to look at a fancy Poodle or a sleek Doberman Pinscher or a flashy Irish Setter. No, Susan Hamil was here to look at a breed that's seldom associated with the glamour of the show ring: a wrinkly, drooling, sad-eyed, long-eared Bloodhound. And she had every reason to believe that one of the wiggling young puppies waiting at the ranch would become one of the greatest show dogs she'd ever see.

"We sat there and ate fried catfish and French fries and watched the puppies," says Hamil. It's arguable that there is no sight on earth cuter than a litter of 2-month-old Bloodhound puppies. They're all wrinkles and round rear ends and ears that they trip over and chew on.

3

Susan felt her heart sing with joy when she saw the big litter of happy, friendly, healthy pups. She knew this litter was no ordinary one. The father of these dogs, Ch. Badger Creek Druid, belonged to her. He was one of the top-winning Bloodhounds of all time, garnering Best in Show wins at prestigious shows over more glamorous breeds. And the puppies' mom, Ch. Ridgerunner Naomi, was no slouch herself.

Like most matings in the world of show dogs, this one had taken place via express delivery. Says Hamil, "You just put the sperm in a tube and send it FedEx." So this was Hamil's first chance to touch the puppies. And she was doing more than just petting them and inhaling the sweet perfume of puppy breath. Hamil was looking at the structure of their plump little bodies, the shape and shade of their eyes, the pattern of coloring on their coats—she was balancing the babies' faults and virtues.

And her eye kept going back to one puppy. "When you get to the level of Westminster, you have to have not only a very outstanding example of the breed, but also that intangible extra something," says Hamil. She was looking for star quality.

There was one puppy who was slightly different from the rest. She had an extra confidence, an extra glow. "You want the dog who stands and surveys her realm," says Hamil. "This is why I chose this puppy over her sisters."

The puppy was promptly dubbed "Fanny"—because of her adorable rear end, and in honor of Fanny Brice, another show girl. Fanny's registered name? Ridgerunner Unforgettable—because of her unforgettable fanny.

WHAT'S WITH THOSE NAMES?

Normal people name their dogs Spot or Lassie or Princess. Or, increasingly, dogs have "people" names, like Chloe or Sophie or Mikey.

Show people give their dogs names like Ridgerunner Unforgettable. Most of their names are even longer—like Charing Cross Ragtime Cowboy. Some even have exclamation points, like Special Times Just Right! Where do these names come from, anyway?

Each dog who is registered with the American Kennel Club has to have a name that is different from any other dog in the history of the AKC. With 1,175,473 puppies registered in the year 2000 alone, it can be a tall order to come up with a simple name that hasn't already been taken.

All show breeders have a *kennel name*. Elaine Woodson, who bred Fanny, is Ridgerunner. Every dog she breeds carries that name. Likewise, Charing Cross and Special Times are the kennel names that have produced some of the top Shih Tzu and Bichon Frises in the history of their breeds. When you see a dog with those kennel names, you know that you're looking at a well-bred dog—maybe even a great one.

A puppy's name often refers back to his famous parents—and their names often refer back to *their* parents. So, the Shih Tzu Charing Cross Ragtime Cowboy is the offspring of Ch. Symarun's Rootin' Tootin' Cowboy and Charing Cross Cyd Charisse—so his name reflects both the Western theme and the musical theme of his illustrious parents. Sometimes the names are just plain humorous. For example, one barkless Basenji was called Ch. Sukari Raider of the Lost Bark.

With breeders trying to fit in their kennel names, references to their canine's ancestors, and the occasional pun, the AKC allowance of 25 letters per name can be woefully inadequate. If you're not careful, the AKC will rename your dog.

When Jerry Elliott and John Wood registered their English Toy Spaniel, they wanted their kennel—as well as that of the co-breeder— to be included in the dog's official name. After much deliberation, Elliott and Wood named their dog Cheri-A Lady Isabella Smokey Valley. But when the English Toy Spaniel's paperwork was returned from the AKC, the last word in her name had been unceremoniously dumped. Now this top-winning little dog is officially known simply as Cheri-A Lady Isabella Smokey.

Breeders often pick a call name that reminds people of the dog's registered name. So, the great Bichon Frise, Ch. Special Times Just Right! is known as J.R.

Ancestor Worship

Leave a baseball fanatic alone, and he'll start playing a game of fantasy baseball. Will the team with Cy Young pitching and Johnny Bench at catcher beat the team with Sammy Sosa and Mark McGwire at bat?

Leave a dog-show person alone, and she'll start fantasizing about pedigrees. What would happen if you bred the grandson of the top-winning dog in the history of the breed with a flashy import from England? Would the genes merge together to make a super dog, or would they meld together to make a dog who looks like he's been designed by a committee?

The dog world, like the horse world, is all about pedigrees. Watch the Kentucky Derby, and it matters that a horse is the descendant of Native Dancer or Alydar—these great racehorses were even more important as sires than they were on the track, because they passed on to their offspring the gift of speed.

And so it is with show dogs. The most important dogs are great in the ring—and then they pass on that beautiful head, the flowing movement, and even the confident attitude of a winner to their progeny. Breeders study pedigrees, keeping thick files of photos of the offspring of key dogs, and dream about a union between a certain dog and a special bitch.

Nowadays, use of fresh chilled or frozen semen is more common than mating the old-fashioned way. Not only can you breed your dog with a famous dog in Japan or South Africa without ever leaving the comforts of home, but you can also breed your dog to one of the famous sires of the breed who's been dead for 20 years. The doggie equivalent of fantasy baseball gets easier every year.

It shouldn't come as a surprise that dog breeders, as a whole, love tradition. The same people who study pedigrees back for 50 years, who have memorized the history and the legends of their dog breeds, whose dogs bear the names of the famous winners of a past generation are the kind of people who love the rituals of dog shows.

And no matter how many breeders scoff that Westminster is "just another show," don't believe it for one minute. Westminster is the mother of all shows. Read the show catalog, and you'll learn where the show has been held every year since 1877—and which dog won, who judged, who owned the winning dog, and who was President of the Westminster Kennel Club that year.

The one sure way for your dog to go down in canine history is for him to make his mark at Westminster. It's the secret thought of every show breeder as she brings a new puppy into the world. It's the unspoken question as a little ball of fluff takes his first unsteady puppy steps. It's the hope and dream when he's 6 months old and is entered in his first local show.

The Westminster Kennel Club show has a pedigree to match the most prestigious puppy.

PICKING THE RIGHT PUPPY

Even with the most scientific approach to breeding, not every puppy in a litter is destined to be a show dog, much less a great show dog.

It's just like human families. The supermodel on the front of *Sports Illustrated* probably has a sister who is just as tall and skinny but has none of her sibling's glamour. Every charismatic politician seems to have a younger brother who is just a likable goofball. Each living creature is an incredible roll of the genetic dice, and not everyone comes out a winner.

Breeders are faced with a tough choice. If a Labrador Retriever has ten well-bred puppies, there's no way to keep all those dogs until they reach 6 months—or sometimes as old as 2 or 3 years—to see whether they're going to develop into show dogs. Breeders would be up to their ears in dogs if they tried that.

Instead, the breeder has to make an educated guess about which dogs she should keep, which she should place in other show homes, and which ones should end up as beloved pets. The dog world is full of stories about breeders who made the wrong decision. There's the top-winning German Shepherd Dog who was found tied up in a backyard, a neglected pet. There's the Miniature Pinscher who was sold as a pet, and when the family decided that they didn't want the puppy anymore, he went back to his breeder—and then continued on to a top-flight show career. There's also the Scottish Terrier, Ch. Gaelforce Post Script (Peggy Sue), whose breeder had carefully evaluated the litter and decided that Peggy Sue and her sister were both show-quality dogs—but that the sister was destined to be the better prospect. The breeder sold Peggy Sue to another dog-show home and kept the sister. The sister never finished her championship. But Peggy Sue won Best in Show at Westminster in 1995.

Breeders hate it when they have to say, "Oops!" They study their puppies from the day they're born. They weigh them, and measure the length of their ears and the ratio between thigh and hock. There's a popular book, video, and seminar produced by AKC judge Pat Hastings called *The Puppy Puzzle*. This package helps fanciers figure out which 8-week-old puppy is going to grow up to be a canine Cindy Crawford or Fabio—and which one will never be invited to the prom.

Amazingly, an experienced breeder with a good eye can usually look at a tiny, formless puppy and, more often than not, accurately predict which one will make it as a successful show dog. It isn't surprising that sometimes the breeder is wrong—what's surprising is that they don't have to say "oops" more often.

Stardust

Star quality, in people or in dogs, isn't just about looks alone. It's often about charisma. It may take an expert in the breed to select for perfect structure and to catch the little flaws that will knock a dog out of the top rankings. But when it comes to that indefinable star quality, everyone can see it.

"When I walk Fanny's niece, people come up and pet her and tell me what a nice dog she is," says Hamil. "But when I take Fanny for a walk, people stop and stare at her."

The nation's top dogs are often described as having a sparkle, an aura, or a special presence. It's similar to Hollywood stars. On film, cameramen have to consider the luminescence of the person on screen. Stars sometimes give off 100 times more light than their doubles. In fact, the very word *star* is all about reflected light.

It's this same luminescence that rivets your eye to top dogs. You can't seem to look away. This is true when you walk the dog down the street, and it's true when you walk him in the show ring. These dogs stop people in their tracks.

Every year, there are maybe two dozen puppies out of a million AKC registrations with this combination of genetics, looks, and stardust. These dogs are the ones who will someday have a shot at getting a nod from a judge in the hubbub and chaos of Madison Square Garden.

But first, these dogs must pay their dues.

On that Texas ranch, eating catfish, Susan Hamil hoped that Fanny would become an unforgettable dog in the history of her breed. Almost exactly four years later, Fanny would succeed in spades.

Chapter 3

Local Shows: A Breed Apart

If this is the middle of July, Jerry Elliott and John Wood know there's only one place to be: Brush Prairie, Washington. "I travel to dog shows every weekend of the year except for two, and those two weekends don't have any shows," says Elliott. Brush Prairie is one of the largest, most prestigious shows in the country. Jerry and John have high hopes at this show for their little English Toy Spaniel, a sweet, friendly dog named Shower (registered as Ch. Cheri-A Lady Isabella Smokey).

Most of the shows that Jerry and John go to aren't the least bit like the hoopla and elegance of Madison Square Garden. They're usually held at county fairgrounds, Elks lodges, or livestock exhibition halls.

The Brush Prairie show is held just a few miles outside of the tiny town of Brush Prairie, Washington, about 30 miles northeast of Portland, Oregon. Forget about the green beauty of the Pacific Northwest: This area more closely resembles the middle of Kansas. The show site takes place in a vast, empty field of farmland. There's hardly a stick of natural shade in sight.

NAKED DOGS AND COUSIN ITT

There's only one reason to gather at this flat little spot in the middle of nowhere: dogs—dogs of such variety and such flat-out weirdness that it's breathtaking.

There are 158 AKC recognized breeds and varieties. The shapes, sizes, and coifs of these dogs are unbelievable. Take the Chinese Crested. These Toy dogs are basically born naked except for small tufts of hair on their heads, paws, and tails. When you see the Toy Group judged, all the other 21 breeds have hair: a fuzzy Pomeranian, a sleek Miniature Pinscher, a sturdy Pug, a silky Shih Tzu. You can't help but wonder if the naked Chinese Crested, surrounded by crowds of people, is afraid he's having some kind of bad dream.

At the show, you can walk past a Puli, a small black dog with its coat formed into long cords. For all the world, this dog looks like Cousin Itt from the Addams Family. Here there are shaggy, gray, Irish Wolfhounds so huge that you can look them in the eye. There are also tiny, sparkling white Maltese, held high above the ground by their handlers so that the rough grass won't tangle their fine coats.

Part of the entertainment at dog shows is human-made: A Poodle's show coat is a sculpted marvel of excess. Show Poodles in full regalia are a sight to see. Their rear ends and legs are shaved to the skin, except for perfectly shaped, round pompons on their hipbones and the tips of their tails, and fuzzy round bracelets of hair on their ankles. In fact, the hair on Standard Poodles is more than a foot long. These dogs resemble a glamorous woman who's wearing a fabulous faux fur coat atop skintight leggings. The Poodle's look is completed when the groomer pulls back the hair around the dog's face into a tight topknot. The wrinkle-smoothing effect of this topknot is remarkably similar to that of a person who's had a facelift.

Human Varieties

At first glance, dog-show people aren't nearly as exotic as their dogs. Folks are overwhelmingly white and middle class; most are middle-aged.

But when you look closer, you see something that you don't see in any comparable sport: Amateurs and pros, kids and octogenarians compete side-by-side.

At a show just a month before Brush Prairie, a child appeared in the ring with his Pomeranian. After the Pomeranian judging was done for the day, the judge kindly explained to the child and his family that at dog shows, Pomeranians are carefully trimmed; their fur is shaped to create an exacting outline. You can't simply bathe your pet and hope to win a ribbon.

At every show, rank amateurs stand in the ring right next to big-time handlers—people who easily net a six-figure income for showing other people's dogs. These handlers bring with them an entourage of assistants and full-time groomers to make sure that their dogs have the best chance of winning.

Stars without the Paparazzi

The USA Network reports that ten million viewers tune their televisions to the cable channel's Westminster broadcast every year. The press is everywhere. However, television crews are seldom seen at local dog shows. There aren't any reporters in sight at Brush Prairie. When local dog shows do get news coverage, it's invariably a light-hearted pet story at the end of the newscast featuring handlers and dogs who look alike.

Dog shows have an aroma of their own, and you can smell it here in the field at Brush Prairie. It's a pleasant, pungent smell of clean dogs, grass, an array of grooming products that cover each dog, and the greasy smell of the food vendors.

In many ways, local shows are more fun than the big show at The Garden. You can see dogs here without elbowing through crowds. The handlers and dogs are relaxed. The top dogs that end up at Westminster in February are out at local shows all year long.

At Brush Prairie, people murmur and point when they see Treasure (Ch. Alabaster Sundown Treasure JH), a long, leggy, ethereal Saluki who won the Hound Group at Westminster in 1999. Ten (Ch. Willow Wind Tenure), the lamb-like Bedlington Terrier that won the Terrier Group at Westminster in 2000, is also at the show. He is among the early, odds-on favorites with a shot at going all the way in 2001.

Seeing these kinds of dogs in the middle of an empty field would be like having the chance to watch Secretariat run around the little dirt track at your county fairgrounds.

◆ ◆ ◆ ◆ ◆ ◆ ◆ ◆ ◆ ◆ ◆ ◆ ◆ ◆ ◆ ◆ ◆ ◆ ◆ ◆

AKC Shows in the Year 2000

- There were 1,409 all-breed shows and 2,044 specialty shows (where one breed or group is judged).
- Shows were held in all 50 states.
- There were 1,524,492 entries in conformation competition.
- 20,588 dogs earned their AKC Championships.
- Shows ranged in size from fewer than 300 competitors to more than 3,000.

◆ ◆ ◆ ◆ ◆ ◆ ◆ ◆ ◆ ◆ ◆ ◆ ◆ ◆ ◆ ◆ ◆ ◆ ◆ ◆

Jerry and John have high hopes for Shower, even with the big-name stars in sight. Shower is an English Toy Spaniel, a perfectly formed, miniature spaniel with a flat face a little bit like a Pug's. Shower has gentle, soulful brown eyes that are always focused on Jerry or John. This year, she's been in a head-to-head battle with an Affen-pinscher to be ranked as the number-three Toy dog in the nation. A big win here just might nose Shower ahead.

PUTTING ON THE DOG

Shower will be shown in one of 19 rings divided from each other with long, flexible fencing. Just like at Westminster, each ring is presided over by an AKC-licensed judge.

Here in the field in the middle of farm country, the judges aren't in black tie or sequined gowns. There's little glamour. And not a penny of old money is in evidence either.

Although you won't see black-tie apparel at Brush Prairie, there is an expectation that people who are showing their dogs in the ring will be professionally dressed. This means a sport coat and tie for men, and dresses or pantsuits for women.

One year, a supportive supervisor came to cheer on his employee, who was showing his Cocker Spaniel. After watching his co-worker show the dog, the supervisor was seething. "We work for a nonprofit mental health organization," explained the supervisor. "For the last four years, I've been trying to get that guy to wear a tie to work, and he refused. He told me he was ethically opposed to wearing a symbol of white male dominance in the workplace. Then I come here, and see him wearing a tie while he runs around in circles with his Cocker Spaniel in the middle of a cow pasture. We're going to have a talk when we get back to work Monday."

The Making of a Champion

There are 11 English Toy Spaniels competing at Brush Prairie, a big entry for the breed.

For most dogs, the goal is to earn a championship. You can tell when a dog has made it: His owner shrieks with joy. People laugh, hug, and kiss. From that day forward, the dog's official AKC name begins with the word *Champion,* abbreviated to *Ch.* It's literally a red letter day, since the dog's name will be written in red on pedigrees— the mark of a champion.

But it isn't easy getting there. *Front and Finish,* an obedience trainers' publication, once did the math: It takes an average of 75 entries to result in a championship. A lot of dogs will be shown most weekends of the year for two or even three years and never earn the necessary 15 points to get their championship.

Brush Prairie is popular because it's a cluster of shows. There are technically four separate dog shows held at Brush Prairie one day after the other for four days. Clusters attract large entries, so it's theoretically possible to finish your championship over the long weekend—that is, if the stars are with you and the judges like the looks of your dog.

◆ ◆

EARNING A CHAMPIONSHIP

- To earn a championship, a dog has to acquire a total of 15 points under at least three judges.

- Points are awarded at the breed level, divided by sex. Males who aren't champions can enter a variety of classes (such as "Puppy, Six and Under Nine Months," "Bred by Exhibitor," or the catch-all "Open"). The winner of each class competes against the other winners for the designation of "Winners Dog." The only male dog in each breed to earn points that day is the "Winners Dog."

- The same process is followed for the females (bitches), with just one female of each breed named "Winners Bitch" and given the points.

- The more dogs you defeat, the more points you earn, up to a maximum of five points at any one show.

- Each dog has to earn at least two *majors*—shows at which he earns at least three points—on his way to his championship.

- The more competition there is in a breed, the more dogs you have to defeat to earn points. For example, a female Labrador Retriever at Brush Prairie would have to be number one among 75 bitches to earn a five-point major. A relatively rare Lowchen would only have to be top dog among six of her gender to earn a five-point major.

◆ ◆

BEST OF BREED

Jerry and Shower wait patiently for their turn. Shower is already a champion, so she shows in the Specials class. Here, the champions of record join the Winners Dog and Winners Bitch for the award of Best of Breed. Shower easily wins the breed. Her day will start in earnest in a couple of hours, when the Toy Group is judged.

Each breed falls into one of seven groups: Sporting, Hound, Working, Terrier, Toy, Non-Sporting, and Herding. The first-place winner in each group contends for the honor of Best in Show. That's the dream for Shower—to win the nod for the best of the best from over 2,700 dogs entered.

We Have Our Standards

How does the judge decide which Bulldog is the most beautiful? And when the breeds are competing against each other for group wins and Best in Show, how does the judge pick between a long, low-slung Basset Hound and a tall, sleek Saluki? Or between a tiny Chihuahua and a hulking Saint Bernard?

The answer lies in the *breed standards*. Every breed has an official standard that is a blueprint of the breed. The standard describes the ideal height, weight, color, head, tail, and even toes of the perfect specimen. Dogs are judged by how well they conform to the standard (which is why it's usually referred to as *conformation*).

The standard also describes the breed *type* (the characteristics that make this breed different from all others). This includes features like a Pug's flat face and wrinkles, or a Bedlington Terrier's lamb-like fur.

In addition to type, the judge will look for *structure* (the dog's physical soundness and ability to do the job he was bred to do). It doesn't do any good for a Doberman Pinscher to have a perfect, chiseled head but a body that isn't athletic and lithe.

Finally, the judge looks at *temperament* (the dog's personality). A shy or aggressive dog, no matter how beautiful, isn't an asset to his breed. Here's where the indefinable—but certainly present—charisma comes in.

In the final analysis, the judge has to decide if the fuzzy, white, prancy, saucy Bichon Frise is closer to his breed standard than the doleful, droopy, drooling, ambling Bloodhound is to her standard. The dog who best displays the whole package of type, structure, and temperament will win.

Conformation shows are often described as beauty pageants. There is a major difference, though: In human beauty pageants, all the contestants look pretty much alike. They're tall, slender, buxom, and leggy. Dog shows, on the other hand, reward an endless variety of shapes and sizes: crotchety Terriers; serious, driven Herding breeds; delicate Toy dogs with paw prints the size of a dime; and massive, impassive Mastiffs with feet the size of a dinner plate. An elegant, leggy, longhaired Afghan Hound just might lose to a broad-shouldered, shorthaired, working dog like a Rottweiler.

Maybe the world would be a smidgen happier if human beauty pageants gave top prize to a chubby, flat-faced, wrinkled woman with a soulful look in her eyes—the human equivalent of a Pug.

Dogs with All Their Moving Parts

The physical examination of a show dog is, well, intimate. There is no other word to describe it. The judge touches a dog—even one with a short, smooth coat—over every inch of his canine physique. The judge is feeling for muscle tone, straight bones, shoulder layback, and correct tail set. Then, at the last moment, the judge gently cups the dog's testicles, making sure each male dog is properly endowed with two normally developed, healthy jewels.

Show dogs are used to this indignity, and they take it with a look of resigned acceptance or slight surprise.

If you're a politically correct pet owner who has spayed or neutered your dogs, it's kind of a shock to go to a show and see intact male dogs. And with some dogs, it's impossible not to notice that they have all their moving parts.

Bullmastiffs, for example, have a lot in common (anatomically speaking) with bulls. And you may find yourself wincing when you see a loose-skinned Basset Hound trotting across the show ring, his testicles flapping in the breeze.

Fanciers explain that dog shows still carry on the tradition of the livestock shows upon which they were modeled more than 100 years ago. The crux of the competition is the evaluation of breeding stock.

Generally speaking, that is what goes on at a show, although there are some exceptions. At shows, some Toy breeds are rewarded for tiny size above all else. If a Chihuahua or a Yorkshire Terrier weighs in at more than four pounds, that dog isn't going to be a big winner. Few tiny females can safely create babies, so larger females are generally bred to tiny males to create the next generation of show dogs. Still, for most of the top dogs in the ring, nearly every dog on the pedigree will be written in red—the indication that the dog is a champion.

All this talk about breeding begs the question: What impact are all these intact dogs having on shelters that are chock full of unwanted animals? The reassuring reality is that serious show kennels have close to zero impact on the massive numbers of dogs—mixed-breed and purebred—that desperately need homes.

Try to get a puppy from a show breeder, and it's almost impossible to get one that doesn't come with a contract containing draconian penalties if you fail to spay or neuter your pet. Show breeders typically breed only their best males to the best females, and waiting lists for their resulting offspring can be years long. Getting into Harvard is a lot easier than qualifying to buy the offspring of a Westminster Best of Breed winner.

About a quarter of the dogs in shelters are purebreds, but almost every one of these dogs was created by careless breeding or by large, commercial puppymills. The likelihood of finding a dog from a top show kennel at a shelter is about as likely as seeing at a dog show a Poodle who hasn't had his butt shaved. It just doesn't happen.

Bitch, Bitch, Bitch

If your mother ever washed out your mouth for using the word *bitch,* a dog show is your ultimate revenge. The "B" word is everywhere.

All the classes are divided into dogs (males) and bitches (females). So it's no big deal for a fancier to say, "Wow, that's a great bitch." And when the female beats out the male in competition, no one blinks an eye or blushes when it's reported that "The bitch went up over the dog."

Bitches in heat can compete at a show. They often sport lined panties, which sometimes come in ruffles or polka dots, to cover indelicate areas when they're out of the ring. It's a courtesy to tell the judge that the bitch is in season before the judge begins to touch the dog all over during the examination process.

There is a lot of controversy about whether bitches have different personalities than dogs. In gleeful disregard of the development of language, fanciers will say with a sly wink, "They're called *bitches* for a reason, you know." (If you think about it, the word *bitch* started out with dogs. It can be argued that humans are called bitches for a reason, while female dogs are called bitches because, well, because that's what they're called.)

Dog-show people are, of course, people who also live and work in the real world. Although they usually don't think twice about complimenting a female dog by saying she is a "stunning bitch," there is still a corner of their brains that laughs at getting away with using a naughty word in polite company.

Want proof? One of the perennial top-selling souvenirs at dog shows are T-shirts ornately decorated with rhinestones that spell out ALPHA BITCH.

Hanging Out at the Show

The entries at Brush Prairie number more than 2,700 dogs. By early afternoon, only the 158 Best of Breed winners—including Shower— are still in competition.

At Westminster, every eye is focused on who's going to win the groups—and ultimately Best in Show. At Brush Prairie, and at pretty much every other show, most of the losers aren't anywhere near the show ring. They're seeking out a little retail therapy from the doggie vendors.

Buy, Buy

The vendors at dog shows sell stuff that's almost as exciting as buying a dog (selling dogs is strictly prohibited at shows). At a major show like Brush Prairie, you can find a dizzying array of collars, leashes, toys, and grooming equipment. But that's just the start. You can also purchase antique dog trading cards that used to come in British cigarette packages. You can have your dog's portrait done—in bronze. You can buy stamps from all over the world with your dog's breed depicted on it (though no one seems to know why Mordovia issued a Papillon stamp).

Show exhibitors often spend more money buying dog paraphernalia at the vendors' booths than they spend on meals, lodging, and gasoline combined.

Wretched Hot Dogs

Most dog-show exhibitors are health-food fanatics when it comes to their dogs. They feed their canine companions carefully formulated foods and are likely to add a brew of supplements—fatty acids, homeopathic remedies, and herbs—to make their dogs look and feel their best.

However, this obsession with nutrition starts and ends with the dogs. Human food is horrendous at just about every dog show in America, and a lot of these people spend 150 days a year at shows, living on this stuff.

It starts in the morning with doughnuts. "You follow the trail of doughnuts, and you'll find a dog show," claims Dominique De Vito, former publisher of Howell Book House and a former *AKC Gazette* editor.

Maybe the doughnuts do something to their taste buds, because dog show exhibitors spend the rest of the day eating the most incredibly bad stuff imaginable—ancient, icky hot dogs that have been circling on a rotisserie for hours; the greasiest curly French fries; dry popcorn, made more palatable with fake butter.

Jane and Michael Stern are food critics; these people know and love great food. They spent a year following dog exhibitors when they wrote *Dog Eat Dog: A Very Human Look at Dogs and Dog Shows*. In an interview, Michael Stern gave his theories as to why the food at dog shows is so awful. "To care about food at all would require exhibitors to take their attention away from winning," says Stern. "You have to be fanatical to love this to the exclusion of everything else. The idea of sitting down to have a delicious meal or even a really good hamburger is antithetical to the passion that the sport requires."

21

Stern has one more theory about why dog-show food is so horrendous: liver bait. Handlers often cram their mouths with over-cooked, leathery, garlic-flavored liver to keep the dog's attention in the ring. "We tasted that stuff. It was really awful. It sure took my appetite away," says Stern, still shuddering at the memory.

RECREATIONAL VEHICLES, KIDS IN CRATES, AND WHO'S SLEEPING WITH WHOM

There are more than 1,400 all-breed dog shows held every year, and the preferred mode of transportation is the RV. Dog shows look like swap meets for RVs: You'll see every model, age, size, and shape, including some pretty slick homemade jobs.

The professional handlers' rigs are pretty understated. They're usually big, long, bus-like vehicles with lots of room for crates and grooming supplies, and comfy beds for the handlers and their assistants. These people are on the road for up to 300 days a year, and their RVs are serious business.

It's the amateurs who have the really cool rigs. They're likely to have air-brushed paintings of the top-winning dogs from their kennels plastered across the side.

Brush Prairie is one of the 25 largest shows in the country. Show organizers have created a little city, and drivers are given directions to park their rigs on Poodle Place, Schnauzer Street, Boxer Boulevard, Akita Avenue, or one of the other makeshift alleyways with canine names.

Each year, up to 1,000 RVs visit the grounds at Brush Prairie. Most of these are festooned with bumper stickers declaring "Dog Is My Copilot," or "A Dog Is for Life, Not for Christmas," "It's Hard to Be Humble When You Own an Ibizan Hound," and even "On the Eighth Day, God Created Irish Terriers."

One very popular bumper sticker announces "The Keys Are on the Front Seat, Right Next to My Rottweiler." However, this popular bumper sticker loses its effect when *Rottweiler* is replaced with *Basset Hound*.

And bumper stickers are only the beginning. The parking lot at Brush Prairie is chock-full of vanity license plates. Many of these license plates declare loyalty to a particular dog breed, such as "LABS," "GOLDEN," "COW DOG," "LHASAS," or "POM MOM." Others are more general, and include "DOGMA," "K9 TAXI," "K9 LVR," "WAGGIN," and "SHOW DG."

At the big shows, RVs are squashed together side by side. Each one is surrounded by exercise pens—portable fence-like enclosures—that are full of dogs. There are grooming tables with Poodles being brushed and primped to the constant hum of hairdryers. Dogs wait patiently in an endless array of wire crates for their turns in the ring. Sometimes kids are in the crates—and parents nervously explain to passers-by that "the kids are just playing dog show—the crates aren't locked." The parking lot at Brush Prairie resembles a third-world slum—except that these people wouldn't move from this mayhem for a million dollars.

The End of the Day

By late afternoon, the dry heat is oppressive. Most of the exhibitors have gone home or are hanging out in their RVs. Inside the relative coolness of the RVs, talk is about all things dog. The tribe repeats stories of their best wins and the great dogs they've known. There's a lot of discussion about the worst dog shows ever. Like the year Brush Prairie was swamped with torrential rains, and the enormous rigs got mired in the field. Or the show in the horse barn, where dogs and handlers had to pick their way through manure left over from a horse show the day before. Then there was the Wenatchee show a few years back: Exhibitors will tell you about a huge prairie fire just a few miles away. Throughout the day's judging, helicopters roared directly overhead carrying giant buckets of fire retardant to stop the approaching flames. But the dog show went on.

There's also plenty of gossip about what goes on at night in these bedrooms on wheels. People talk about which handlers are sleeping with each other, which handler is sleeping with his assistant, and which handler is sleeping with her groomer. There is also a lot of guessing as to just who is straight and who is gay. Because most people at show dogs are decidedly middle-aged, you can't help but wonder if life in these RVs is only half as exciting as the rumors suggest.

BEST IN SHOW

Shower has stayed in Jerry and John's van all afternoon. They leave the engine running so the air conditioner will keep Shower cool and comfortable. "The van's only two years old," says John. "We've put 140,000 miles on it—and every one of those miles has been to dog shows."

The Toy Group is called. Jerry likes to be in there first, letting Shower lead the way among the other little dogs. He has high hopes for today. It's the second day of the four-day cluster, and Shower won the Toy Group the day before.

Shower looks good. Jerry unbuttons his jacket; it's hot. He sprays water into Shower's mouth to keep her cool. "You're always anxious. There's so many little things that you can't take into consideration," says Jerry.

Jerry and John have been scoping out the competition all day. They know just which dogs have won each breed—and which favorites were upset by which young upstarts. "It's mean and vicious to say, but sometimes when a top dog gets beaten in the breed, you get help but say, 'Yeah!'" admits John.

Tonight, there are some great dogs in the ring. Jerry and John are hopeful. The judge is Kenneth McDermott, who has bred Brussels Griffons, a flat-faced breed with similarities to an English Toy Spaniel. "He understands the Toy Spaniel, maybe more than some judges who don't have a personal background in the Toy breeds," says Jerry.

The judge carefully looks at Shower, and then looks closely at another dog. He has the two little dogs gait for him one last time. Jerry and John can hardly breathe.

The judge then places Shower in the front of the line of dogs and instructs the handlers to circle their dogs around the ring as a group.

"One. Two. Three. Four," the judge says as he points to the first four dogs in line.

Shower is the top Toy dog at the show for the second day in a row.

"That's the best we could have hoped for," says Jerry. What he couldn't have dreamed was that there was more to come.

Brush Prairie is one of the most competitive shows in the country, and the really big names are out in full force. The Best in Show judge this evening is Gerald Schwartz. "We didn't think we had a chance," explains John. Schwartz mostly judges Sporting, Working, and Herding breeds. Judges with that kind of background and preference usually aren't going to pick the Toy dog.

Still, despite the heat, which is especially hard on a flat-faced dog like Shower, the little dog is in a great mood and is showing especially well. Her gait is far-reaching, like a tiny Sporting dog. Her face is cherubic.

Schwartz carefully examines each dog. He has them gait individually and together. He weighs the faults and virtues of every one of these seven top-winning champions.

"Standing there with Shower, I knew the judge was looking at us," says Jerry.

Then judge Gerald Schwartz deliberately walks over to the table in the corner of the ring, writes down a breed and a number, and walks back into the ring with the red, white, and blue Best in Show ribbon.

The dog he points to is little Shower.

"I was absolutely shocked," says Jerry. This was Shower's fourth Best in Show win, breaking the all-time record for Best in Shows for any English Toy Spaniel in the history of the breed. And this wasn't a Best in Show at some tiny little outpost of dogdom—this was a huge win at one of the most prestigious shows in the sport. "I'd waited for that moment—that exact moment—for 20 years of showing dogs," says Jerry.

There will be more shows during the next six months, but there is no doubt about it: Shower is headed to Westminster.

Chapter 4

Judging: When Beauty Is in the Eye of the Beholder

For a year and a half, Kent Delaney had to keep a secret.

It couldn't have been easy for this talkative, popular man. But he didn't tell a soul about the most important honor he'd ever been given in his life.

Kent Delaney was tapped to judge the Hound Group at Westminster in 2001. The judging assignments for the show are made two years ahead of time, but they are a tightly-kept secret until the Westminster Kennel Club makes the announcement eight months prior to the show. Being asked to judge a group at the show is one of dogdom's top honors. With ten million television viewers—not to mention the serious dog fancy—second-guessing your choices, it's certainly the most visible job any judge will ever have.

Delaney, a retired journalism teacher, is an energetic man who seems to wear a perpetual grin. He's been coming to dog shows since he was a kid. "My parents showed Boxers," he says. "I came to shows for the ice cream." Delaney's love affair with ice cream matured into a love affair with dogs. For the past 30 years, he's been one of the fancy's most respected and popular judges.

In an interview at a local dog show in Washington State, Delaney admitted that he was a bit nervous about doing the assignment under the constraints of live television. "They have very strict timelines. I might have a problem getting my judging done on time," he admits.

Delaney abruptly stops the interview when a man with a Basenji walks past. He gently touches the man on the shoulder and says, "I just wanted to say to you that your dog was beautiful. When he gets a little older, he's going to do really well." The man smiles enormously, thanking Delaney for his comments. Dog show judges don't have to go out of their way to encourage an exhibitor, but it comes naturally to Delaney.

He turns his attention back to the interview.

"When you're invited to judge at Westminster, they just send you a letter, saying you've been selected to judge. They don't ask if you're free that day. They assume that you are," he says, smiling again.

Delaney relishes judging. He smiles with obvious joy when he touches a great dog and watches him move.

Given the amount of whining and complaining about judges at every dog show, it's a wonder that anyone signs up for the job at all.

POLITICS, PAY-OFFS, AND BLIND JUDGES

Go to any dog show anywhere in the country, and you will hear one word on the lips of the exhibitors: politics. People coming home from their first show might think the whole event was rigged—a canine version of professional wrestling.

When a gangly puppy loses to a polished champion, the puppy's loving owner is likely to shake his head and snarl, "Politics." When a judge *puts up* (awards a win to) a dog who's handled by a professional handler, someone will mutter, "Politics." And when a dog who's owned by an AKC-licensed judge wins, people ringside will look at each other in silence and raise one eyebrow, communicating that unspoken word: *politics.*

It would be disingenuous for a book about show dogs and dog shows not to mention the "P" word.

There's nothing that causes more complaining, more rancor, and more indignation than the judging at a dog show. Once at the Vancouver Kennel Club Dog Show, a red, second-place ribbon was torn to tiny pieces and scattered on the cement floor of the fairgrounds building. Show ribbons are sturdy—it took someone white-hot with anger to make this mute testimony to what he thought of the day's judging.

A dog show isn't like a horse race or a hockey game or a pole vaulting competition. It isn't merely a matter of going faster, or getting more pucks in the net, or jumping higher. Although the breed standards give an objective description of the ideal dog, the interpretation of that standard is highly subjective. And that's where all the trouble starts.

Other sports with subjective judging criteria deal with the problem by assigning a panel of judges to each competition. Go to a gymnastics tournament, an ice-skating competition, or a ballroom-dancing competition, and you'll see a whole row of judges, whose scores will be averaged. Some competitions even knock out the low and high scores, just to take away any possible taint of politics.

Even a criminal gets a jury of 12 people to determine his fate.

Until 1929, panels of from two to ten judges decided most of the Westminster Kennel Club Best in Show awards. However, that practice has long since been discontinued. Currently, only one judge reigns supreme in each show ring.

Judges certainly aren't in it for the money: The maximum a show pays is about $500; some pay a lot less. The Westminster Kennel Club doesn't pay judges a cent, except for lodging or travel expenses.

Two Minutes a Dog

At every show, whether it's televised or not, judges are allotted approximately two minutes per dog for judging. A class of 15 dogs will take a half hour to judge; a class of 2 will take about four minutes. During that time, the judge has to give each animal a thorough going-over, looking at the dog and feeling him. The judge has to determine how well the dog conforms to the breed standard from his teeth to his tail set, from the length of his ears to the shape of his toes. The judge has to decide which dog has more virtues than the next, placing the top four animals in each class in rank order. He has to sort all that out, despite the fact that one dog may be expertly handled by a top professional in the sport, while the next dog is inexpertly handled by someone who's never been in the ring before. It's a daunting task by any measure.

If you've entered a dog, two minutes certainly doesn't feel long enough for any judge to appreciate your dog. Just getting to a local show requires hours of work and preparation. There's the travel time, not to mention all the hours spent grooming, hair spraying, chalking, and trimming your dog to make him look like a sculpted marvel. There are the added expenses of a professional handler, a hotel room, and meals made up of greasy dog-show food.

You do all this, and what you get is two short minutes during which the judge examines your dog, weighs all his faults and virtues, and compares him to the other dogs in the ring. It's easy to believe that your dog got short shrift, and occasionally, you may be right.

In the Eye of the Beholder

Most of the controversy about judges happens because, deep in your heart, you believe that your dog is the most beautiful creature on four legs. You have a picture in your mind about what a great dog of your breed looks like, and it's not a coincidence that this picture looks a lot like the dog on the end of your leash.

The judge also has a picture of the perfect dog of your breed in his mind, but this picture might be radically different from yours. While you see your dog as "fine-boned, light, and dainty" as required by the standard, the judge just might see him as spindly. While you think your dog's gait has fabulous reach and drive, the judge might think the dog is just kicking out his front legs in a parody of the correct movement. You think your dog is muscular while the judge thinks he's muscle-bound.

On the day of the show, the judge's opinion is the only one that counts.

This leads to a lot of bad feelings, and a lot of complaints.

"You bring your dog in the ring because you think he perfectly reflects the standard," says one long-time exhibitor. "When the judge disagrees, it hurts your feelings."

It's kind of like hearing someone say your child is ugly.

And so, when their dogs lose, people complain that the judge is blind, stupid, crooked, or sleeping with all the other competitors. "People's egos run away with them, and they just can't help themselves," says Michael Stern.

HOW TO WIN FRIENDS AND INFLUENCE JUDGES

Because it's a subjective sport, people will do everything they can to have judges select their dog over all the others in the Group and Best in Show rings.

One strategy? Advertising.

There are dog-show magazines that look like the canine equivalent of *Vogue*. These are big, slick 'zines that contain page after page of ads, many in full color, interspersed with an occasional article. The top dog show 'zines are *The Canine Chronicle, Dogs in Review, Dog News,* and *ShowSight Magazine.*

Cover dogs grace the fronts of these magazines, every bit as much the professional as Cindy Crawford or Elle MacPherson. The cover dog strikes a model-like stance, posing in front of idyllic scenery, her flowing hair groomed to perfection. In the same way that supermodels want to be on the cover of fashion magazines, it's a big deal for a dog to make the cover of a show magazine—especially just before Westminster.

Instead of flashy ads for Gucci or Chanel, when you flip though these magazines you'll see advertisements boasting the latest wins of America's top dogs. A typical ad shows a dog with his handler getting a Best in Show ribbon at a prestigious event under a famous-name judge. "Thank you!" reads the ad, giving the judge credit for his great taste.

Dog fanciers pay big bucks for this kind of exposure. Color ads with plum placement can run more than $1,000. Advertising is one of the biggest expenses in campaigning a show dog, with owners of a top-name dog often paying $60,000 a year in advertising expenses alone.

You'll find free copies of *The Canine Chronicle, Dogs in Review, Dog News,* and *ShowSight Magazine* at the big shows, as well as on the coffee tables of every serious fancier—and every judge. Subscription rates vary from $48 to $150 a year. Or, if you're an AKC-licensed judge, they will be sent to you for free.

Winning at dog shows, the thinking goes, is just like anything else. Name recognition helps. You want the judge to recognize your dog and handler as a winning package when they walk into the ring.

"It's just like car dealerships or anything else," says Tom Grabe, publisher of *The Canine Chronicle.* He points out that his company also produces magazines for show horses and racehorses, and that advertising is part of the business of any high-stakes sport.

"Some people in the dog fancy have a misconception that advertising makes dogs win. You can't advertise a bad dog and make him win. But you can take a good dog, advertise a lot, and make him into a great dog," says Grabe.

Advertisers say that exposure creates a level playing field among competitors. When a dog from Minnesota competes in California, the California judge will feel the same familiarity with an out-of-state dog that he feels with a local dog.

This familiarity, argues Grabe, can translate into a better show career. "It becomes a tie-breaker," says Grabe. "Maybe even subconsciously the judge knows that the dog has a Best in Show or has won under a respected judge like Anne Rogers Clark. It won't make a bad dog get a Best in Show win, but it might tip the judge's decision between two good dogs. It also might make the difference between getting a group one rather than a group two, or getting a group four instead of not placing at all."

Since *The Canine Chronicle* first came out 26 years ago, advertising has become a matter of course for top dogs. The last Westminster Best in Show winner who didn't advertise was owner-handler Chris Terrell, who won with the Afghan Ch. Kabiks The Challenger in 1983. Even then, it was considered daring to forego the edge that advertising could give the dog.

No one knows how much advertising pays off in Best in Show wins. In the same way that Coke and Pepsi aren't going to take a chance by *not* advertising, neither will the owners of top dogs.

For the average dog fancier, it's fun to settle down with one of these glossy magazines and enjoy the beauty of the dogs, just like it's fun to read the ads in *Vogue*. But make no mistake about it: This is business. "Nobody advertises in the magazine just because they want to see a picture of their dog," says Grabe.

However, an ad occasionally touches your heart. It might be a picture of adorable puppies touted as the next generation of champions from a famous kennel. It might be the retired show dog hunting in the field, showing that the breeder's line can still do what the breed was meant to do.

Sometimes, the ads are just a way of saying thank you to a dog who has shared the life and love of the breeder who cherished him. Black and Tan Coonhound breeders Jim and Kathy Corbett wanted to pay tribute to their dog Boomer (Ch. WyEast Why Not) when the old dog died. The Corbetts wanted this great show dog's friends and fans to see him one last time. So they ran an ad, showing the dog in his prime, blissfully baying up a tree, with the simple caption, "Happy Hunting, Boomer." Every once in a while, the ads aren't about business at all.

EXTREME MEASURES

One of the great bones of contention in the dog world is the exaggeration and the changing styles of show dogs. When you go to your local show or watch Westminster on television, some of the dog breeds are hard to recognize compared with your pooch at home.

Like Paris fashions, show dogs are sometimes harbingers of what your breed will look like in the future.

Some of the exaggeration is superficial, like the Poodle's show coat. Originally, Poodles were retrieving dogs and their masters cut some of the hair off their rear ends to make the dogs less heavy in the water. These early sportsmen left tufts of hair on ankles and hip bones to protect the Poodle's joints from chilly waters. Over time, that clip became more stylized and exaggerated, and much more showy.

Today, Poodles are shown in the Continental clip, in which their rear end is shaved to the skin. Until about 30 years ago, Poodles were routinely shown in the English Saddle clip, which leaves a fuzzy blanket of hair across the rump, giving the breed a much less exaggerated look. When the Continental clip came into vogue; handlers of those dogs sniffed, "I don't have to hide my dog's rear from the judges." Other handlers then had to prove that their dogs' hindquarters were just as attractive, so they shaved their dogs' rears, too. Today, you never see a Poodle shown in an English Saddle clip, despite the fact that dogs with both clips should—in theory—be judged equally.

But hairstyles in dogs, as in humans, come and go. You probably giggle at the hairstyle you wore to the junior prom. The same goes for show Poodles. When a Poodle's show career is over, he's trimmed into a short, comfortable, low-maintenance utility clip. His hairstyle during his show career, no matter how exaggerated, doesn't make any difference in the long run.

Other exaggerations are much more controversial. Dog shows are a competitive sport. If there is a little hair on a winning dog, then more hair must be better. If long legs are good, then longer legs must be better.

It's amazing how quickly the body type of a breed can change. Take Cocker Spaniels. In 1940 and 1941, Ch. My Own Brucie won Westminster twice in a row. He epitomized the perfect Cocker for the time: sturdy, with a moderately long nose, medium-sized eyes and moderate amounts of hair feathering his legs and tummy. In 1954, a Cocker Spaniel again won Westminster, Ch. Carmor's Rise and Shine.

You would hardly recognize this dog as the same breed that had won just 13 years before. The winning dog's nose was snubbed, and he had big, round eyes and large quantities of hair billowing from his tummy and legs. Cocker Spaniels made a permanent transformation that changed the breed for all time. There are no more Cockers who look like My Own Brucie—they all have the shorter nose and more profuse feathering that came into vogue after his win.

On the other hand, some appearance changes come and go. A decade ago, many winning Irish Setters were all hair. Very often, these dogs were scrawny specimens who had lost the look of a sporting dog—their bodies were just frames for their flowing, red tresses. But today's top-winning Irish Setters look much more like hunting dogs: slightly sturdier, stronger, and less exaggerated. More often than not, the fancy pulls itself back to the origins of the breed.

Today, there is increased emphasis on the working nature of dogs. There is a whole slew of activities, including hunt tests for Sporting dogs, lure coursing trials for sight hounds, earthdog tests for Terriers and Dachshunds, and Herding titles for the sheep and cattle dogs. More than ever before, it's considered prestigious for your dog to have both working and conformation titles. These working titles are a major force against exaggeration. Too much hair or a clumsy body just doesn't cut it in the world of a working dog.

Of course, the exaggeration of type is in the eye of the beholder. The coat that one person decries as an abomination on a Sporting dog is seen by another as a beautiful asset to the breed. The nose that one person sees as ridiculously pointy is elegant to another.

Exaggerated fashions in dogs are a lot like the changing image of women's appearance in the media. Everyone decries the fact that Hollywood stars are getting skinnier and skinnier every year. Still, try to find a starlet who's willing to go to an audition weighing 20 pounds more than the others; she's not going to risk losing her chance at a role because she looks different than everyone else. The same is true in the ever-changing face of dog-breed fashions.

The Renaissance Man

In the world of show judges, Kent Delaney is a dual expert: He's one of the nation's top judges in both obedience and conformation. In fact, the national rankings of obedience dogs are determined by the Delaney system—invented by Kent Delaney.

Delaney says that judging and competing in obedience influences how he looks at dogs in the conformation ring. "A good obedience dog has to be structurally sound," says Delaney. These dogs have to jump over hurdles. They need to nimbly drop to the floor, then on a signal, get up and run toward their owners. If they have structural problems, they won't last in competition for long.

Conformation judges have to weigh *structure* (physical soundness) against *breed type* (the unique characteristics of coat, body shape, expression, and other features that set one breed apart from all others). Some judges narrow the competition down to the dogs with the best breed type, and then look at structure. Delaney says that he narrows down the competition by first selecting for good structure, and then picking the dog with the best breed type among those dogs.

"A lot of breeds go through phases of exaggerated style," says Delaney. "I'm more moderate. I want the dog to have the structure to do what he was originally bred to do." He thinks for a moment, then smiles. "I don't want the dog to be ugly. I just don't pick a dog simply because she's cute or pretty."

Of course, in the Hound Group at Westminster there will be plenty of dogs with both fabulous structure and great breed type. There will also be elegant dogs of great style—without exaggeration.

Kent Delaney has a reputation for loving dogs, and he's eager to be surprised by a wonderful new dog he's never seen before. Forget the glamorous ads in the slick magazines. Forget the grooming that's designed to hide a dog's flaws. Forget the whining that's bound to happen when your dog isn't picked. Kent Delaney has a job to do, and he'll do it with honesty, conscientiousness, and care. That's the kind of judge he is.

"I just hope I can do it in the time they give me," he frets.
In any event, he's on his way to Westminster.

◆◆◆◆◆◆◆◆◆◆◆◆◆◆◆◆◆◆◆◆◆◆

AKC JUDGING QUALIFICATIONS

Dog-show judges start out as long-time breeders and exhibitors. As of June 2001, the basic requirements to receive approval to judge your first breed were:

- At least 12 years experience in the sport
- Bred or raised at least five litters in the initial breed to be judged
- Bred at least four champions in the breed
- Volunteered as a ring steward at shows and judged at *sanctioned matches* (practice dog shows)
- Passed written tests
- First five judging assignments observed by AKC officials to ensure competency
- Approval to judge additional breeds requires more tests and proof of knowledge of the breed

◆◆◆◆◆◆◆◆◆◆◆◆◆◆◆◆◆◆◆◆◆◆

Chapter 5

A Rhinestone Cowboy and Hocking Mama's Jewels

Ch. Charing Cross Ragtime Cowboy doesn't look like he'd put fear into the heart of big dogs. Joey is a Shih Tzu with long, flowing hair. He wears a precious, green bow in his topknot that sparkles like a tiara. This little dog has bright, dark eyes, a black button nose and a Kewpie-doll mouth. Joey's name might be "Cowboy," but he's strictly of the rhinestone variety.

You might be tempted to underestimate this little dog. That would be a big mistake. At the highest levels of dogdom, Joey is a star. He's not just the top-winning Shih Tzu of all time; he's the top-winning Toy dog who's ever pranced across the planet.

Joey belongs to long-time breeder, exhibitor, and philanthropist Gilbert Kahn. Even Kahn can't believe his luck in having bred and owned a dog like Joey. "You get a dog like this once in a lifetime," says Kahn. He knew from the beginning that Joey had the potential for greatness. "I have a picture of Joey at 1 day old," says Kahn. "He had such a beautiful head." Gilbert Kahn should know what it takes to win at the top. More than anything else, Kahn is a dog man.

DOGS FROM THE INSIDE OUT

Gilbert Kahn is a polite man. He's careful, almost courtly, in his speech—until he starts talking about dogs. Then the words come so quickly that they almost trip over each other. It's impossible to really keep up with what he's saying.

Kahn talks about Joey and the dog's pedigree, and the pedigree of Joey's son, who's just beginning to rip up the show circuit. This philanthropist, who could be spending his time jet-setting around the world attending parties in Monte Carlo, cares deeply, completely, passionately—and compassionately—about dogs.

Over the years, many wealthy people have thrown money at show dogs or dabbled in the sport briefly. But Kahn is the real deal; he knows his breeds inside and out. In fact, Kahn is a sought after Best in Show judge—not just in the United States, but all over the globe. "I'll be judging this year in Australia, Japan, and Finland," says Kahn. And then he starts talking about his good friends in the dog world in each of these countries, and how anxious he is to see them again.

Serious dog people don't care whether you're a blue-collar worker or an heir to a fortune. When they talk about dogs and pedigrees and the time they won Best in Show or were unceremoniously dumped, the lines of the rest of society are blurred and forgotten. All that matters is whether you know dogs.

It all started for Kahn at the Westminster Kennel Club Dog Show in 1952. Like hundreds of thousands of other people over the years, Kahn came to look at the dogs and think about the right breed for him. He fell in love with a Norwich Terrier that day and became a highly regarded breeder.

In the 1970s, Kahn acquired some Japanese Chin and Shih Tzu (the plural of Shih Tzu is *Shih Tzu,* and the plural of Chin is *Chin,* just like the plural of sheep is *sheep*). Soon, Kahn was one of the most respected names in those breeds.

"The big thing at Westminster is to win the breed," says Kahn. And he did it once before, with another Shih Tzu. But that dog's record was nothing like Joey's. Of course, there's never been a Shih Tzu in history with a record like Joey's.

THE PERFECT MATCH

There are a lot of reasons why Joey is considered a nearly perfect Shih Tzu. First of all, there's his gorgeous head. Also, by a fortunate quirk of nature, Joey was born with dark eyebrows on his cream-colored face; when his hair is pulled up in a topknot, these dark brows form into long, black arrows pointing directly towards Joey's black button nose and adorably pouty mouth.

But Joey is more than just a pretty face. This Toy dog moves like a Sporting dog, with a ground-covering gait that's thrilling to see. When Joey gaits, his long coat flows like a waterfall. You can't take your eyes off him.

Show dogs don't go into the ring by themselves. They aren't statues or oil paintings, sitting still for everyone to admire. These living, breathing, tail-wagging works of art need a handler in the ring who knows how to make them look their best.

Enter Luke Ehricht.

"I thought of Luke right away," says Kahn, who knew that Joey should be in the hands of one of the best handlers. "I've known Luke since he was 15 years old."

Luke Ehricht has a Shih Tzu pedigree as distinguished as Joey's. He's handled Toy dogs—especially Shih Tzu—at the top level for years. His wife breeds top winners in the breed, and her mother bred them before her. There was no doubt about it—Luke was the guy to guide Joey through his life as a show dog.

Sometimes It Pays to Hire a Trained Professional

When you go to a dog show, or watch one on TV, showing a dog doesn't seem that difficult. The dog trots around the ring, he stands still for the judge to examine him, and then he trots some more. This doesn't take the brains of Rin Tin Tin.

But it's not nearly as easy as it looks.

Just like a great jockey makes a horse run faster, a great handler makes a dog look better. "You can ride your own horse in the Kentucky Derby, but it would be foolish," says Susan Hamil, who owns Fanny the Bloodhound. Just as there are legendary jockeys, there are also legendary handlers. Names like Peter Green, James Moses, Andy Linton, Bruce and Gretchen Schultz, Bill and Taffe McFadden, Luke Ehricht, and Scott Sommer are as familiar to the dog-show set as names like Eddie Arcaro, Bill Shoemaker, Pat Day, and Jorge Velasquez are to the racehorse set.

With a few rare and notable exceptions, dogs who rank in the top 20 almost always have professional handlers. Typically, these dogs live with their handlers for two or three years during their show careers. If you want to be an Olympic gymnast, odds are you'll leave home as a preteen and live with one of the world's top coaches. If you dream of being America's next Queen of the Ice, you'll go find the best coach you can—even if you're 13 and must move to a foreign country. And if you want to have one of the nation's top show dogs, you'll almost certainly send him off to live with one of the nation's top professional handlers.

A great handler does a thousand little things at every show to give his dog an advantage. Before he ever takes a dog into the ring, there's extensive preparation. Joey's coat takes hours to groom. It can take 20 minutes to position, tease, and beribbon his topknot alone. A careless snip of the scissors on his long, flowing coat could set back Joey's career a year.

Even short-coated breeds take preparation. At one summer show, a woman who handled her own dog was grumbling that a big-name handler had won the breed every day for four days in a row. "It's just so political," she said, giving her dog a pat. A small cloud of dust rose up from the dog; he was covered with dirt from spending four days at the gritty fairgrounds. Contrast this with the professional handler's dog who gleamed in the summer sunshine, clean and seemingly polished. The handler and his staff had bathed and groomed every dog in their care every morning of the show, something the amateur had never thought of doing.

Then there's the training. "Every dog has a balance point," explains professional handler Andy Linton, who has shown a Doberman to Best in Show at Westminster, and is a perennial winner year-round. Linton says that once you find that balance point, you train the dog to hold himself where he looks his best. When one of Linton's dogs is in the ring, the animal is the epitome of polish: trained, conditioned, poised, and impeccably groomed.

Dog showing is a physical sport, especially if you have a big dog. A professional must have the wherewithal to run in the ring with a German Shepherd Dog, or to make minute adjustments to match the stance of a tiny Yorkie.

Showing a dog is similar to being the male ballet dancer who supports the prima ballerina, or the straight man in a comedy team. These are the quiet roles that no one particularly notices—but if these folks aren't smart and skilled and capable in their own right, the whole routine will fall apart.

Most of all, a really good handler knows how to make the dogs in his care happy. "Luke loves Joey, and Joey loves Luke," says Kahn. That relationship between dog and human is all-important. If a dog doesn't feel comfortable, safe, and confident in the ring, he isn't going to win that day. Watch the top show dogs—they're all having a tail-wagging good time.

For three years, Joey was in Luke Ehricht's care. He slept in Luke's bed. He followed Luke from room to room, and from place to place. When they flew to shows, Joey never once went in the cargo hold—Luke lovingly carried him onboard in a specially-made, ventilated bag that fit snugly under his seat.

When they left the show ring, Luke would sweep the little dog up into his arms and give Joey a kiss. There was undeniable love between handler and dog.

"A really good handler has knowledge of nutrition, veterinary issues, and behavior," says Susan Hamil. She remembers the day that her handler, Gretchen Schultz, called. One of Hamil's Bloodhounds had just won a Group First at a show—but instead of celebrating, Gretchen was worried. "He just seems a little off," she said. The judge hadn't noticed anything—neither had anyone else. But Gretchen took him to a veterinarian right away. Sure enough, the dog had a bladder infection and was promptly treated.

If you wonder whether there's a bond between a show dog and his handler, just ask Andy Linton. Linton is a slim, athletic man who reminds you of the Dobermans that he often handles. Like a Doberman, Linton can seem just a little aloof. "I'm not a very emotional guy," he says. Until he starts talking about dogs—dogs he handled in the past, and dogs that he handles now. Linton is being interviewed at a local show, and he absently pets an American Foxhound that he's showing. Linton looks down at the dog's gentle brown eyes and asks, "How could you not love a dog like this?"

Linton admits that there have been a couple of dogs especially hard to return to their owners at the end of the dog's show career. "I know that their owners love these dogs, and that the dogs will have happy lives as family pets," he says. But he'll still miss having the dog in his life. Linton admits that his eyes sometimes fill with tears when he hands a dog back to his owner.

A great handler understands a dog's soul.

The Owner-Handler: A Rare Breed

Black and Tan Coonhound breeder and exhibitor Kathy Corbett is so well-known on the show circuit, that they call her "Kathy Coonhound." Corbett and a handful of other owner-handlers succeed side-by-side with the professionals. Her WyEast Coonhounds have amassed 20 Best in Show wins, and have been Best of Breed winners at Westminster seven times.

Corbett is clear that there are advantages and disadvantages to showing your own dogs. "I learn something every time I go into the ring," she says. "Handlers do, too, and they go in the ring hundreds of times more than I ever do." Corbett has great respect for the outstanding handlers. She also points out, "They don't have day jobs; this isn't a hobby for them."

A successful owner-handler has to devote pretty much every weekend of her life to showing her dog. She has to have the physical ability and grooming know-how to show the dog to his best advantage—an easier task with a small, smooth-coated dog like a Miniature Pinscher than with an athletic, extensively groomed breed like a Standard Poodle.

But there are advantages to showing your own dog. "I have one dog to think about, train, and condition," says Corbett. "When I go to a show, I can give my dog my complete concentration." A professional handler, who may be showing ten dogs or more, has to divide his time—and his focus.

The dog fancy holds the outstanding owner-handler in great respect. "When I'm in the Best in Show ring, and I'm the only owner-handler there, I know I've got a shot at it," says another breeder-owner-handler. In a sport that considers itself a family activity, it's always a popular win when the judge gives the nod to a person who has bred, raised, and shown a dog to the very top.

For the breeder-owner-handler, showing a dog is a special, even profound experience. "When I show my dog, I see his grandfather's legs," says Corbett. "I see his mother's eyes looking at me."

When she wins, Corbett finds that she has a ritual. "I sink to my knees, hold my dog's head in my arms, and I say 'Thank you, thank you, thank you.' We are a team, and we won together."

Treasure: She Gave Me Wings

Karen Black says that her dog Treasure was her answer to menopause.

Treasure (Ch. Sundown Alabaster Treasure JC) is the top-winning Saluki of all time. This creamy-white, long-legged sight hound has soulful brown eyes. And these eyes are always focused on Karen.

"Showing Treasure is exactly what it would be like to be taken in Fred Astaire's arms and danced across the floor," says Karen. Indeed, when you see the two of them in the ring together, it looks like a dance. Treasure, slender and elegant, runs gracefully and proudly in front, her lead loose. Karen, tall and slim, runs behind her, smiling with joy as she watches her dog move.

"In the ring, it's Zen," she says. "I don't feel the arthritis in my knees. I don't know there's a crowd. It's a state of meditation. Treasure has 100 percent of my attention."

In the world of dog shows, "Karen and Treasure" are always spoken like one word—Karenandtreasure. Sort of like the inseparable couple you knew in high school. "Did you see Karenandtreasure? Didn't they look wonderful?" "Do you think Karenandtreasure are going to take Best in Show?"

And Karen Black wouldn't have it any other way. You see, Treasure changed her life, her relationship with her family, and, most of all, the way she saw herself.

For more than 30 years, Karen and her husband Darrell, a veterinarian, raised top quality Salukis. They'd had other dogs who had taken Best in Show wins at prestigious dog shows. Always, it was Darrell who showed the dogs, while Karen was their support system.

Now, with her children grown, Karen Black was looking for something to call her own. "The children needed to know my emotional well-being wasn't dependent on them. I needed to separate," she says in her quiet, thoughtful tone.

And then Treasure came along.

Karen showed the puppy in a few fun matches (practice dog shows) and realized that she wanted to show this dog herself.

Karen even created an image of herself to reflect Treasure. She always wears black and cream-colored clothes to be a counterpoint to the dog. Karen's blond hair is now carefully coifed. "I'd always just pulled it back in a ponytail," she says with a laugh. But Treasure's elegant look required that Black mirror her elegance back.

When Treasure decided that she didn't like flying, Karen drove her to every dog show—even across the country. When Karen's husband can take time off, they travel together in a refurbished Greyhound bus—replete with all of the family's Salukis and cats. But most traveling involves only Karen and Treasure in a minivan together.

"Winning and losing doesn't matter," says Karen, "as long as we do it together."

For five years, this team did a lot more winning than losing. Treasure won the Hound Group at Westminster in 1999, as well as Hound Group seconds in 1998 and 2000—along with a lot of notable all-breed and specialty shows in between.

Karen Black became one of the most recognizable figures in dogdom. She and Treasure have been the cover girls for many dog magazines. When the fancy wants to prove that an owner-handler can be just as successful as a top professional, they point to Karen Black.

Karen says that success has improved her longtime marriage to her husband. "I'd devoted my life to enabling him to succeed," she says. "I've learned that being valued and respected in my own right is more valuable to him. He's gotten a lot out of it."

Black gently strokes Treasure's silky ears, and runs her hand down the hound's long, graceful neck. Her eyes misting, Karen says, "Treasure gave me wings."

What You Need Is a Sugar Daddy

The cost of showing a dog at the elite levels is staggering. The price tag for a campaign can top $200,000 a year. And top dogs are usually campaigned seriously for about three years. This adds up to a lot of kibble.

Top handlers can charge $30,000 a year for showing a dog. Then there's room and board and traveling expenses, not to mention $60,000 a year in advertising in the dog magazines. There are a lot of stories about dogs who took chartered jets from one show to another so they wouldn't be subjected to the indignity of traveling by cargo.

It doesn't take long to run into serious money.

Dog showing can be a struggle for middle-class people. There are many sad tales in the show world of people who mortgaged their homes or hocked their family's treasures to give a dog a shot at the big time. Since, typically, the only prize for winning Best in Show is a huge red, white, and blue ribbon—or maybe a silver bowl, a crystal vase, or a Pendleton blanket—it's never wise to spend money that you don't have on a show dog.

Still, middle-class people can and do figure out ways to show their dogs, even at the elite level. "When we decided to really go for it with Shower, we sat down and planned it out," says Jerry Elliot. Shower (Ch. Cheri-A Lady Isabella Smokey) was the number one English Toy Spaniel for 1999 and 2000. Much more impressively, she was the number-four-ranked Toy Dog in 2000. Elliot makes a living selling (mostly canine) collectibles, and he can't write out an endless supply of checks. "We sat down and decided to show her, knowing we could have spent the money paying off a substantial portion of our mortgage instead," says Elliot.

Dog showing on a budget means thinking about which shows—and which lineup of judges—are going to be the most favorable for your dog. It means catching the red-eye to save a night's lodging expense, or sharing a room with a friend—or three or four. You need to time your advertisements in the show magazines carefully, so judges will be reading them just prior to the show that you hope to win. Sometimes you can trade favors in exchange for a deal with your handler; you'll puppysit the handler's brood bitch and brand new litter, if he'll handle your dog for free.

But everyone dreams of a backer—a canine sugar daddy.

The Backer

A *backer* is someone who's willing to write checks supporting a dog and footing bills for handling, advertising, and travel—the kind of edge that can catapult a dog to the top.

This has to be a special kind of person. Backing a dog isn't like investing in the stock market—or even like gambling in Las Vegas. There's not a chance that you'll ever make your money back. A backer writes checks for the sheer pleasure of helping a dog amass the show record that he thinks the dog deserves.

Dr. William Newman co-owned the great Alaskan Malamute Ch. Nanuke's Take No Prisoners, who won the Working Group at Westminster in 1998. He also backed Ch. Whipperinn's Virgil J, the top-winning English Foxhound of all times.

"I don't like the word *backer*," says Newman. "It sounds like you're producing a Broadway show." Newman is a tall, elegant, retired radiologist who looks like a TV doctor, with his chiseled face and friendly demeanor. "I like to call it *sponsoring* a dog. It's like a local company that sponsors a softball team or a peewee football team."

These people are similar to art patrons. Just as an art lover might support a museum so that the general public can enjoy it, a backer may sponsor an outstanding dog so that he can be seen at shows. "A sponsor wants a really fine dog to be seen by the world," says Newman.

Every once in a while, a millionaire who isn't from the doggie set decides to back a dog—or he meets a breeder who talks him into it. More often than not, this Johnny-come-lately soon tires of the sport. Most backers resemble Newman, who is a serious devotee of the sport of dog shows. He's bred his own Mastiffs for 40 years, and judges several breeds.

"Besides," says Newman, "it's an ego trip. Dog shows are extremely competitive. It's fun to win, and to know that you helped a dog to win."

Lassie Has Four Mommies

Flip through a dog-show catalog and you'll see that most dogs have two, three, four, or more owners. Breeders, backers, and even trainers and handlers sometimes all co-own a dog with the person who actually purchased the puppy. It's more confusing than a modern suburban family.

Although co-ownership is the norm among show-dog owners, it can be fraught with peril and bad feelings. Think of it as a marriage. When co-ownership works, it's great. The dog has a team of people who provide the expertise, the finances, and the bond of trust that supports the dog in her quest for the top.

Unfortunately, co-ownership, like marriage, doesn't always work. In fact, it's enough of a problem that the American Kennel Club actually warns against the practice. The AKC cautions in a policy statement: "Co-ownership arrangements, in far too many cases, lead to problems. While AKC registration application forms provide for more than one owner, **we recommend that co-ownerships be avoided,**" even putting the warning in boldface.

When these relationships fall apart, it can get ugly. At the root of the problem is the fact that, although these dogs are valuable, they are more than just property. There's love, pride, ego, and disappointment involved when these close relationships go sour. There are tales of shouting matches, fistfights, and even dog-nappings—situations not so different from those that people find themselves in when they're arguing over custody of their children.

Ch. Loteki Supernatural Being was the subject of one of these custody battles, which was fought in the courts in Connecticut not long before the 1999 Westminster show. The court eventually gave custody of the dog to co-owner John Oulton, who was required to pay breeder and co-owner Lou Ann King a reported $40,000. When the little Papillon won Best in Show at the 1999 Westminster show, it was Oulton who captured the glory as the dog's sole owner.

Making a Living

All the money that people spend at shows goes somewhere. Professional handlers aren't the only people who make a living from dog shows; it's an entire industry. There are professional groomers who specialize in the show cuts of labor-intensive breeds like Bichon Frises, Poodles, or Terriers. These folks deftly wield scissors that can cost as much as $800 a pair, as they coif dogs' coats into sculpted perfection.

There are full-time doggie travel agents, who make dog-friendly flight and hotel arrangements for exhibitors and judges. Shows are organized by AKC-licensed superintendents. The superintendent's staff puts out a comprehensive show catalog, reports the results to the AKC, and makes sure that protocol is followed to the letter—from the playing of a scratchy tape of "The Star-Spangled Banner" to the awarding of Best in Show. Most shows require complicated parking schemes to fit the RVs into the space at the county fairgrounds, and people earn money organizing the parking.

High-tech dog sex requires a frozen semen bank—and companies such as the International Canine Semen Bank (ICSB) fill this need. Someone printed a bumper sticker that you'll see at shows proudly proclaiming: "My Dog Banks at the ICSB: First in Frozen Assets."

Dog-show photographers make a living taking photographs of dogs' wins. Another group of people design the layouts for advertisements in dog magazines.

Show vendors and catalogs tailored to the dog-show crowd sell specialized crates, doggie hairdryers, boar-bristle brushes, and leads to be used only when the dog is in the ring, along with hundreds of other products designed to give a dog the winning edge. And don't forget the doggie press, from pet columnists for local papers, to the staff of show-specific magazines like *The Canine Chronicle,* and the general public magazines like *Dog Fancy,* all of whom make money off the dog-show business.

Make no mistake about it: Dog shows may be a hidden culture that goes mostly unnoticed by the rest of the world, but a lot of people make a living from them. Dog-loving lawyers have given up their practices, corporate executives have quit the rat race, wives have divorced their husbands—all to seek work in the canine-related professions, where a person can earn a living with her pooch at her side. There are thousands of ways that people have carved out lives for themselves with dogs in mind. Sometimes these lives are marginal, but sometimes they are quite profitable.

GIVING BACK

While the amount of money that's spent campaigning a dog can be dizzying, there's another side to the money equation of the dog fancy. The odds are pretty good that one of the owners of a top show dog will save the life of your pet one day. That's because no one contributes more to canine health care than the purebred show fancy.

Gilbert Kahn, for example, hasn't forgotten that the life of every pet is just as precious as the life of his show dogs. Through his family's charitable foundation, Kahn has endowed the deanship of the University of Pennsylvania School of Veterinary Medicine. This medical school conducts research in fields such as genetic disorders, hip dysplasia, and critical care and behavior. Kahn has given personal funding to research on epilepsy and diseases of the central nervous system. He has also donated generously to many other causes, including veterinary school scholarship funds and the Animal Welfare Society of South Florida, which sponsors a low-cost spay/neuter program and a complete veterinary hospital.

Dr. William Newman doesn't just write checks to sponsor his favorite dogs, either. Instead, he gives generously of his time and money to the Canine Health Foundation (which conducts research into canine genetic diseases) and many other canine health causes.

Rescue Me!

You don't have to be a jet-setter to make a difference. Susan Hamil's husband, John, is a veterinarian. This pair of devoted dog lovers gives plenty of their time to Bloodhound rescue.

Purebred-dog rescue volunteers are mostly devoted breeders who want to make sure that every dog of their chosen breed has a loving home. When someone can't—or won't—take care of a dog, purebred-dog rescue takes over. They'll provide foster care for a homeless dog, nurse him back to health, and then match him to an ideal family—taking his physical and emotional make-up into account.

Ironically, dogs who are bred by people like John and Susan Hamil don't end up in purebred rescue. Ethical breeders will always take back a puppy if the buyer can't keep him—even if the "puppy" has grown into a 10-year-old adult dog with health problems. The dogs in purebred rescue tend to be from commercial breeders who sell dogs to pet stores. Or they are from people who thought they could make a little money by breeding their family pet—and would never think of tracking a puppy throughout his lifetime.

Dr. John Hamil volunteers his veterinary services to Bloodhound rescue below-cost. Each dog is spayed or neutered before being placed in a new home. While the dogs are under anesthesia for their spay/neuter surgeries, Dr. Hamil X-rays the dog's hips to determine if the animal has hip dysplasia.

"We've found that about 60 percent of the dogs in rescue have hip dysplasia," says Susan Hamil. "The rate of dysplasia among carefully bred Bloodhounds is about 20 percent." The X-rays ensure that rescued Bloodhounds will get appropriate medical care. Equally importantly, they prove the value of carefully screening dogs for hip dysplasia before they are bred. That's good for every dog—and for the people who love them.

Dozens of Causes

There are countless good causes that grab the attention of the dog fancy. There's the Canine Health Foundation, which does groundbreaking research into the causes of canine disease. There's Take the Lead, which provides financial assistance to people in the dog fancy who are facing life-altering illnesses. And there's more: local humane societies, independent shelters, veterinary schools—the list is endless.

ON HIS WAY

Every day, the fancy gives to its charities, has its squabbles, and worries about the cost of showing dogs.

But all that is forgotten when autumn comes, and the invitations to Westminster are about to be mailed. It's a time of excitement, promise, and dreams.

And one little rhinestone cowboy, with his sparkling ribbon, his bright eyes, and his movement like a Sporting dog, just might take the whole thing. Joey the Shih Tzu is on his way to Westminster.

◆ ◆

GETTING MONEY BACK

In a surprise announcement in May 2001, the American Kennel Club said there would be large cash prizes at the AKC Invitational dog show to be held in December 2001. Sponsor Iam's dog food will give $50,000 to the Best in Show winner, and $25,000 to the breeder of the Best in Show winner. There will be significant cash prizes for group placements and Best of Breed wins, as well.

This is a major change in the sport of dogs. AKC Board member Patti Strand points out, "You can get $180,000 for winning a bass fishing tournament."

Time will tell if other shows follow suit.

◆ ◆

This giant inflatable dog, the mascot of the Iams Company, is a clue that something unusual is going on at the Hotel Pennsylvania. © *Deborah Wood*

The 2001 Westminster issue of *The Canine Chronicle* features Joey (Ch. Charing Cross Ragtime Cowboy) the Shih Tzu, one of the favorites going into the show. Magazines like *The Canine Chronicle* are thick and glossy and have the slick feel of a fashion magazine such as *Vogue* — but for the doggy set. © *The Canine Chronicle/ Courtesy of Tom Grabe*

A number of competitors at Westminster excel in events such as lure coursing, agility, herding, and obedience. Dual Champion Classic's Can Do Andrew is a champion in field trials, and won awards of merit at Westminster in 2000 and 2001. © *Jim and Julie Brown*

Ch. Sundown Alabaster Treasure JC, and owner-handler Karen Black, in the Hound group at the 1999 Westminster show. "Showing Treasure is exactly what I imagine it would be like to be taken in Fred Astaire's arms and danced across the floor." © *Michael Ross, Ross Photo*

Here is Fanny (Ch. Ridgerunner Unforgettable) all grown up and winning the Hound group at Westminster in 2001. © *Ashbey Photography*

Shower (Ch. Cheri-A Lady Isabella Smokey Valley) has a happy moment with owner-handler Jerome Elliott on the day that she won Best in Show at Brush Prairie. No matter how hot the day is, male handlers are required to wear a coat and tie into the ring.
© *Diane Heston, Riverdog Photo*

Mick (Ch. Torum's Scarf Michael) won Best in Show at Crufts, the British Westminster. He also won Best in Show at the 2000 Morris and Essex Kennel Club Show, and then won the Terrier group at Westminster in 2001. But could he go all the way and win Westminster? © Ashbey Photography

The Bichons are on. © Dominique De Vito

Ch. Royal Tudor's Wild As The Wind UDTX (Indy) won Best in Show at Westminster in 1989. She went on to become one of the country's top performance dogs, earning a Utility Dog obedience title and a Tracking Dog Excellent title. © *Cheri McNealy/ Courtesy of Susan Korp*

When Arlene Cohen dressed her Field Spaniel, Henry (Ch. Marshfield's Boys' Night Out), in a yarmulke and side-curls, it changed her life. © *Ashton Larsen, The Picture People*

Compared to the mobs of people at Westminster, a crowded shopping mall at holiday time is roomy. This is the West Highland White Terrier judging at the 2000 Westminster. © *Deborah Wood*

Ch. Flatford Zeus The Major God, JH, the Flat-Coated Retriever who won the Sporting group, was a crowd pleaser at the 2001 Westminster. © *Ashbey Photography*

Show dogs often don elaborate outfits to protect their precious coats. This dog models a lycra bodysuit from K9 Top Coat. © *K9 Top Coat*

The crowds at Westminster are thicker than on the New York City subway at rush hour. © *Janine Adams*

Ch. Lajosmegyi's Dahu Digal, a Komondor, created quite a stir at the Westminster Kennel Club show in 1993. Dahu's hair was formed into 2,774 cords that weighed 19 pounds. © *Carl Lindemaier, Animal World Studio*

JR—Ch. Special Times Just Right! — the animated Bichon Frisé, who likes to clap his paws together, is crowned top dog at the 2001 Westminster Kennel Club show. © *Ashbey Photography*

Chapter 6

The Dogfight for Number One

••

They call it a campaign. Like a series of offensive battles in a war. Like a brawling political contest that spans the country.

The campaign to be the number-one dog in America is a grueling, exhausting fight, and it leaves only one dog at the top.

In 2000, the dog who ranked number one in the ratings was a saucy Bichon Frise called J.R. In those 12 months, J.R. (Ch. Special Times Just Right!) amassed one of the best records in the history of dogdom. "We got 77 Best in Shows and 158 group firsts," says professional handler Scott Sommer. He estimates that J.R. was in about 170 shows, since there were a few shows in which J.R. didn't win the group.

A dog doesn't get a record like this if he doesn't love being a show dog. "J.R.'s never had a bad day," says Sommer. "He's just extremely happy 24 hours a day." J.R. is known for waving his front paws when he's happy, and he's happy almost all the time. J.R.'s a little Energizer Bunny of a dog. "He's every dog handler's dream," says Sommer. "He's never, ever, ever let me down."

You don't talk to Scott Sommer for long before you realize that he loves this dog. J.R. sleeps in Scott's bed at night. "J.R. follows me everywhere I go. I'm in the house, and he's with me. I'm down at the kennel, and he's with me." Then Sommer will tell you how smart J.R. is, how quickly he learns things, and how, although he might look like a fluffy, pampered pet, J.R. is a great companion for a guy.

FROM ONE GENERATION TO THE NEXT

Getting to number one requires a team. "You need a great dog. You need a great owner. You need great people working for the handler," says Sommer. "I couldn't do this without my assistants."

Even at the highest levels of the sport, working as a handler isn't the way to make an easy buck. The dogs have to be fed, exercised, and trained to show. They need play time and affection. They're bathed and groomed every day at every show—and a handler typically has about 20 dogs in his care at any given show.

A handler isn't going to succeed if he doesn't have a capable, hard-working, dedicated staff. "I have three terrific guys who work with me. They're learning to be handlers," Sommer says. These young men are in their late teens and early twenties. While most guys their age spend weekends hanging out with friends and partying, Scott's assistants work 12– and 13-hour days at dog shows.

Professional handling isn't something you learn by taking college classes or reading a book. It's something you learn by working side-by-side with someone who does it successfully. All the tricks and all the lore are passed along from one generation to the next.

"I worked for Michael Kemp," says Sommer. "He passed on the stories, how to care for dogs, how to condition them, how to look at them, how to understand them." Sommer is passing these skills on to the next generation. "You have your reputation, and you can't let it slide. I just work and work and work and work. I learned how to do this from someone who was the same way."

Among elite handlers, dogs always come before people. If you're up all night driving to a show, the dogs must be fed, exercised, and bathed before any human can get to sleep. "They're not paying us to do it any other way," says Scott. "The dogs need to be walked or run three to five miles a day. They need to be groomed properly. The only way to do this is the right way."

To see J.R. win at show after show, week after week, it all seems so easy. Just like a great ballerina makes balancing on the tips of her toes seem natural, Scott Sommer makes showing this cheerful Bichon seem like an effortless walk in the park.

At the end of the year, Sommer and J.R. are cruising along in first place in the standings. Joey the Shih Tzu—with 52 Best in Show wins—is holding on to second place in the standings. He has just nosed out a foxy-faced Pembroke Welsh Corgi named Ch. Coventry Queue.

A NATIONWIDE CHESS GAME

By late summer, owners and handlers are making strategic decisions that will gain them the most points in the standings. In the Hound Group, Fanny the Bloodhound was in a heated battle with a Black and Tan Coonhound named Ch. Southchase's Warrior Princess (Xena) and the English Foxhound Ch. Whipperinn's Virgil J (Virgil).

"Toward the end of the year, we really wanted to be the number-one Hound," says Fanny's owner Susan Hamil.

The strategy: Go into the Coonhound's territory. If you beat her on her own turf, you get the points for the rankings, and she doesn't. Still, it was a strategy that could backfire. "Taking on your competition head to head is a risky thing," says Hamil. "The top hounds are all really beautiful dogs." Fanny could lose against the competition just as easily as she could win—and go home with nothing to show.

Still, the lure of the big shows in Boston drew Fanny's team. The more dogs you defeat, the more points you earn in the rankings. And there weren't a lot of big shows in California at that time of the year. To really go for the gold, Fanny needed to be in Boston.

"We took Fanny from California to Boston twice at the end of the year," says Hamil. This was a big decision to make when you have a dog who weighs more than 100 pounds. Fanny can't ride in the cabin like Joey the Shih Tzu or J.R. the Bichon can.

Airlines don't make it easy for dogs like Fanny to travel. Big dogs have to fly in the cargo hold. Suddenly, during hot summer months or cold winter weather, airlines began restricting the ability of dogs to fly on the same flight as their handlers. Then United Airlines stopped accepting dogs as checked-in baggage altogether. They would only take dogs sent separately as cargo, if the shipper was a "known entity."

The bottom line was that puppy mills could still ship dogs long distances without anyone on board to care for them, while a professional handler or an owner couldn't even be sure that his dog would be on the same plane. The purebred dog fancy found these changes both upsetting and incomprehensible.

Luckily, Fanny was able to fly with her handlers without incident, but every trip was a worry. And there are other things they would rather worry about.

When handlers scramble for rankings, they look for judges who are likely to favor their dogs. "There are some judges who, for whatever reason, just don't care for your dog," explains Hamil. The pros know which judges are likely to give their dogs the nod—and which ones are likely to give their dogs a thumbs down. "To win a Best in Show, the moon and the stars have to align," says Hamil. "You need the right breed judge, the right group judge, and a Best in Show judge who will look at your dog."

The stars aligned on those trips to Boston. Fanny came home with key Best in Show and group wins. She was the top Hound in America. Fanny had momentum going into Westminster.

The British Invasion

By early autumn, the Westminster picture looked pretty clear. The top dog was clearly going to be J.R. the Bichon. In every other group, competing dogs were sorting themselves out.

Then something happened to change everything. In one single day, J.R.'s was no longer the name on everyone's lips.

Mick (Torum's Scarf Michael), a Kerry Blue Terrier, came to the United States in June and began showing in September. In the eyes of the dog fancy, he was the hottest British import since the Beatles—well, at least in the dog world.

Mick won Best in Show at Crufts, England's answer to Westminster, in March 2000. Then his owner and breeder, Ron Ramsay, decided he wanted Mick to have a chance to make history. Ramsey got the word out that he'd like to see Mick come to America. He wanted to see if Mick could be the number-one dog on both sides of the Atlantic.

Marilu Hansen bought Mick. There's a lot of speculation as to how much money Hansen paid for Mick, but she politely—and adamantly—won't tell. The most Hansen will say is that she paid "more than a dollar" for Mick.

Hansen is proof that watching a television program can change your life. In 1988, she watched the Westminster dog show on TV, and decided then and there that she wanted to get involved. "I'd been a veterinary technician and had done dog rescue," says Hansen. But she had never set foot at a dog show. In 1994, Hansen bought her first show dog, a Giant Schnauzer. Her second show dog, another Giant Schnauzer, Ch. Skansen's Tristan II, was one of the top dogs in the country in 1999.

Mick was her new project. Teamed with Hansen's handler, Bill McFadden, Mick started showing in September.

Although Mick was England's top dog, he'd never set a paw on American soil and wasn't an American champion. Not a problem. Mick earned his American championship in three straight shows, going Best in Show at each one.

The American Kennel Club doesn't keep records, but no other dog in memory has ever accomplished such a feat. This achievement wasn't lost on the dog show scene. Everyone wanted to see Mick. They wanted to touch him. They wanted to watch him move. And they wanted to see him make history.

Between shows, Mick was busily siring puppies with select bitches. Part of his breeder's dream is to improve American Kerry Blues with Mick's vigor and quality.

At a cluster of shows in Portland, Oregon, in January, the owner of one of the Kerry Blue bitches that had been bred to Mick had her first chance to see him up close and personal.

"Can I touch him?" she asked handler Bill McFadden in a tone barely louder than a whisper.

McFadden is a friendly guy, and he brought the dog over for her inspection. As the woman touched Mick's fur, she got a dreamy look on her face. Afterwards, she beamed with joy as she described the encounter to her friends. "That coat doesn't hide anything," she said. This is a big statement, since elaborate terrier trims are often used to disguise flaws in a dog. She explained that Mick's neck fit perfectly into his shoulders, and that his shoulders flowed perfectly into his body. He was strong and athletic.

One friend asked, "So, did you check out his testicles?"

The woman blushed and nodded. She cupped her hands in a generous fashion. "He's perfect," she said, sighing.

Mick's owner, Marilu Hansen, makes it clear that she doesn't consider herself an expert on Kerry Blues. She says she just wanted to make sure that Mick had the chance to come to the United States and make his mark in dog history. Hansen says that the old-time Kerry Blue people say he's the best dog there's ever been.

Kerry Blues were first bred in Scotland at the turn of the century as an all-purpose farmers' dog. Larger than most other terriers (about 19 inches at the withers and weighing about 35 to 40 pounds), these dogs hunt vermin, herd livestock, retrieve game, and are also known as wonderful family pets.

Mick looks like a dog who can do all that. He's well muscled and sturdy. The true test of a dog's structure is his gait, and Mick's ground-eating trot is breathtaking. He moves with a breezy, athletic gait that makes other dogs—even other great dogs—look slow and ungainly by comparison.

If you've ever wondered whether a dog has charisma, you haven't met Mick. Mick's soft, sculpted gray coat gives off an aura of light. Walk into a crowded dog show full of a couple thousand dogs, and you can find Mick just by the light he gives off, like a big-time preacher or politician or movie star.

Ramsey sold Mick to Hansen on the condition that he be a family pet, not just a show dog. So Mick now lives in the house with professional handler Bill McFadden, his wife Taffe (who is one of America's top handlers in her own right), and their three kids. "Mick has a regular, everyday life that involves children and other pets—even a cat," says Hansen. "He's Bill's companion all the time." People who went to the prestigious Montgomery show at the beginning of October were as impressed with how well Mick played with the McFadden kids as they were with his win over the nation's other top Terriers.

From September through January, Mick rarely failed to bring home a Best in Show. The stage was set for a showdown at the Garden.

The Dream of Being #5

For most dogs, the goal isn't to be the number-one dog in the country, or in the group, or even in the breed. It's to be number five in your breed. Five is the magic number that gets you invited to Westminster.

THE INVITATION

For the first 123 years of Westminster, owners desperately tried to get their dogs into the show. In recent years, Westminster resembled a rock concert that sold out in a matter of hours. If your entry didn't arrive in the first two hours that entries were open, your dreams of glory were over. Frantic exhibitors mailed, faxed, and messengered their entries (and sometimes did all three), hoping to ensure that their dogs would make it. Some top dogs' entries didn't get there in time. Sometimes entire breeds weren't represented at the show.

For the 2000 Westminster, the policy changed radically. The top five dogs of each breed were invited to the show. The rest of the available entries would be on a first-come, first-served basis.

Owners are on the Internet daily, checking to see which dogs are winning and how their dog is faring. If a couple of other dogs have a great weekend, your champion can be knocked down from number three or four in the breed to the heartbreaking position of number six.

Then, one day in October, the envelope arrives. The return address is the Westminster Kennel Club. It's the letter that tells you your dog has been invited.

Does the number-five ranked dog of an obscure breed have the chance to win Westminster? Not really. If your dog hasn't beaten a dog like J.R. the Bichon or Mick the Kerry Blue in a hundred shows, he's not likely to beat these dogs at The Garden.

For most of the dogs at the show, just like most of the competitors at the Olympics, the thrill is just being there, participating, seeing how your dog stacks up against the best his breed has to offer.

Still, every exhibitor can't help but dream.

And the handlers of the nation's top dogs can't help but worry. Westminster is called "the giant killer." About half the time the number-one ranked dog wins the show. And half the time he doesn't. Dogs have been plucked from relative obscurity into the shining light of Best in Show.

Going in with momentum helps, but it's no guarantee that you'll win. You might not even win your breed. That's The Garden for you.

So 2,500 dogs and their handlers, owners, groomers, friends, and entourages are headed for Westminster.

One of them was going to win it all.

I WANT A DOG JUST LIKE THAT ONE!

The stakes are high for everyone involved in a Westminster win. It's a huge coup for the handler, who can be sure that his phone will ring off the hook with people who want him to show their dogs. The breeder and owner are held in huge respect throughout the purebred dog world. The winning dog retires to a happy life of hanging around with the people who adore him; if the Best in Show dog is a male, he'll spend a significant amount of time siring puppies. Everyone comes out a winner—except, perhaps, the breed.

Winning Westminster can skyrocket a breed's popularity. The most famous Westminster winner of all time is still probably Ch. My Own Brucie, who won Best in Show in 1940 and 1941, and is widely credited with catapulting the Cocker Spaniel to the top of the popularity charts.

History may be repeating itself. A little Papillon with the impressive name of Ch. Loteki Supernatural Being (called "Kirby") has been a Westminster star twice. In 1996, he won the Toy Group and the hearts of many viewers. He won Best in Show in 1999, and he did it in a prancing, joyful, confident, look-at-me style that brought this obscure breed to the attention of the world.

Since Kirby first came into the national spotlight, the number of Papillons registered with the AKC has nearly doubled. This is a worry for people who love the breed. Popularity—especially sudden popularity—isn't good for any breed.

Papillon fanciers, who have done a wonderful job producing healthy, happy dogs and matching them with the right homes, fear unethical breeders will breed dogs just to produce puppies. Papillons occasionally appear in pet-shop windows, where anyone with a credit card can purchase them—whether or not he's the right owner for this busy, active, small-boned breed. The number of dogs finding their way into the Papillon Club of America rescue program is mushrooming.

In 2001, a new dog will win. Thousands of television viewers will instantly fall in love with the breed. Responsible breeders will be ready for the avalanche of calls from people who want a dog just like the one who won Westminster.

JUNIOR SHOWMANSHIP: IT'S A FAMILY TRADITION

It's not just the dogs who are vying for number one. It's also the kids.

Every dog show is populated by dozens of kids dressed just like adult business people. The boys have their hair neatly slicked back; they wear crisp white dress shirts and a sports jacket or suit. Their silk ties are carefully knotted. The girls wear slim-fitting two-piece suits, and invariably have their hair in French braids.

In the world of dog shows, these 10– to 17-year-olds are incredibly hip. This is what the doggie teen set does on weekends—they compete in the some of the toughest competition of the day: junior showmanship.

Some juniors learn about showing dogs through the great dog 4-H program that's open to kids from all walks of life around the country. But most of the competitors were born to the dog-show life, with parents or grandparents who are breeders, judges, or even professional handlers.

Junior showmanship competition focuses entirely on the handler. Kids are judged by how well they present the dog whom they bring into the ring. If a dog is exuberant, the judge will watch to see how the junior settles the dog. If a dog is slow-moving, the judge will watch to see what the child does to bring animation to the creature.

Similar to the way that top dogs are ranked by their wins, kids who compete in junior showmanship are in a flat-out race for national rankings. If you win at least eight junior showmanship open-class competitions, you can enter Westminster. This is a goal that some kids—and some parents—have from the time the child is a toddler.

Winning Before Most Kids Can Spell *Dog*

Make no mistake about it: These kids are excellent handlers, often at an incredibly tender age. "My grandma has Toy Poodles. I showed her dogs in the regular classes before I was 10 and could enter junior showmanship," says Eva Dawson, who went to Westminster in Junior Showmanship in 1998, 1999, and 2000. (Her sister Jennifer showed at the 2000 and 2001 shows.)

In what has to be an all-time record, professional handler Scott Sommer started showing his mother's Smooth Fox Terriers before he was in kindergarten. At the incredibly young age of 5, he showed a dog to a championship. While other kids were still playing in the sandbox, this young boy could present a dog to his best advantage, breezing past adults with decades more experience.

Candice Walker made it to Westminster for the Junior Showmanship competition in 1996, 1998, 2000, and 2001. In 1998, at the age of 14, she flew from the West Coast to Westminster by herself, bringing her own Dalmatian to show in juniors, and an English Toy Spaniel called Faith (Ch. Fairoak's Face the Music) to show for a woman in breed competition. While Candice didn't get selected for the finals in showmanship that year, she successfully handled Faith to Best of Variety. "It was a total shock," remembers Candice. With the optimism of youth, Candice had packed an outfit to wear in the televised group competition. "I had on a long, cream white dress with a short jacket with sequins. I even wore little heels. I looked like I was 26," remembers Candice, laughing. When she gaited the dog in the group competition, television host David Frei told the audience that Candice was just 14, and a junior handler. Then he read from his notes, "Candice has been handling dogs for 12 years."

Most of the top juniors are the children of professional handlers or work for them. They can earn somewhere between $20 and $70 a day doing the dogs' basic grooming, making sure that the right dog is ready at the right time and in the right ring with the right armband. In a pinch, an experienced, older junior will show a dog in the breed ring if the professional handler can't get back in time. "I got a Group Second with a Portuguese Water Dog," says Eva Dawson.

When Dogs Save Your Life

While junior showmanship is a lifestyle choice for most kids, a fun activity for some, and an obsession for others, it was a lifesaver for Candice Walker. Her mother and stepfather, says Candice, "had personal problems." Candice focused her energies on her Dalmatian,

Magic. "After school, I'd go out to the track with Magic. I wanted to be a really smooth handler. So we'd run lap after lap together, until I was moving with him the smooth way I wanted to." She says she won the award of Best Junior Handler over 350 times with Magic during a five-year period.

Candice left home when she was 15. "That was the year my grandmother died, and everything really fell apart. For a while I felt like there was nothing. I had no place to go," she says. At the time, she was working for professional handler Ellen Cottingham; Ellen offered Candice a home.

Three years later, Candice credits Ellen for the wonderful changes that have happened in her life. "Ellen has done more for me than anyone I know. She's taught me how to be a livable person, a human being, a lady. She's been a mother to me. She's taken me under her wing and guided me through. I don't know why she ever did it. I don't know why she wanted to take on that responsibility."

By her sophomore year in high school, Candice was taking high school classes through an independent study program and working for Ellen full time. In junior showmanship, she was racking up wins with a yellow Labrador Retriever named Baron. Candice made it to the finals in junior showmanship at Westminster with Baron in 2000, and showed him to four Group Firsts at other shows.

That success in the show ring, coupled with the lessons she's learned from two-footed and four-footed friends, has made all the difference. Candice has come a long way. She was a kid from a troubled family who could have become a troubled adult in her own right. At 18, Candice is a pretty woman, with an open, friendly face and an athletic, graceful build. She's among the most popular people at dog shows, greeting everyone with a huge smile and a hug. Candice is not sure where her future will eventually take her—most likely, professional handling. She just graduated from high school, and thinks about taking some college courses, possibly in child psychology. "I understand what kids go through," Candice says. But she is sure of one thing: Dogs will always be part of her life.

Weddings, Babies, and Broken Majors

Dogs have always been a part of Christina Marley's life. Christina won Best Junior Handler at Westminster in 1992. This funny, friendly woman with girl-next-door good looks is now a professional handler. When she got married three years ago, there was only one place to hold the ceremony: at a dog show. Christina doesn't see this as unusual. "It was the only way to get all my family and friends in one place," she says. A judge presided. "He wasn't a 'regular' judge," Christina says. Then she clarifies, "I mean, he wasn't a dog-show judge."

When Christina went into labor with her baby boy, it was also a dog-show event. "I couldn't believe it—there was a major in Irish Setter bitches," she says. Majors are a big deal to dog-show people. To complete a championship, every dog has to earn 15 points. The more dogs he defeats at each show, the more points he earns, up to a maximum of five points. A dog has to earn at least two majors along the way—where he earns at least three points. Majors are hard to find and important to win.

And Christina had the bad luck to go into labor on the day of a major in her own dog's breed. To make matters worse, there were exactly the number of entries required to make a major. Christina had to withdraw her dog and deliver her baby. Without Christina's dog, the show would no longer be a major.

"I called everyone from the hospital, telling them I was so sorry I had to break the major," she says. Christina sees the humor in the situation. "Life's gone to the dogs when you're more worried about breaking the major than you are about labor pains," she says with a laugh.

Christina's adorable little boy comes with her to dog shows. Most likely, he'll belong to the next generation in the dog fancy.

Meanwhile, there were 121 junior handlers entered in Westminster in 2001. And every one of them dreamed of doing just what Christina had done in 1992: winning the award for the Best Junior Handler at the world's most prestigious dog show.

◆◆◆◆◆◆◆◆◆◆◆◆◆◆◆◆◆◆◆◆◆◆

GETTING TO NUMBER ONE

The goal is to be number one in the rankings for your breed, your group, and—the highest level—all dogs.

- Dogs are ranked in their breeds by the number of dogs *of the same breed* they beat in competition. If your dog wins Best of Breed with a total entry of ten dogs, he'll earn 9 points (for the number of dogs he defeated). If he wins Best of Breed with an entry of 100 dogs, he'll earn 99 points.

- The five highest-ranked dogs in each breed *in breed competition* are invited to Westminster.

- Dogs are ranked in group and all-breed systems by how many dogs of all breeds they beat. For example, if a Collie wins Best of Breed with an entry of 10, he earns 9 points; if he goes on to win a Group First at the show with a total entry of 450 Herding dogs, his total goes up to 449; and if he wins Best in Show with a total entry of 2,500 dogs, he'll add 2,499 to his total points. This dog would have earned just 9 points in the *breed* standings; but 2,499 in the *group* and *all-breed* rankings.

- The dog who won second place in the Herding Group would accrue 438 points in the rankings (since he beat all the other Herding dogs except the winning Collie and the other Collies in the competition).

- Some top-winning dogs, especially of rare breeds, could fail to qualify for Westminster even if they win several Best in Shows. If you have the only American Water Spaniel in a show and then win Best in Show with an entry of 1,000 dogs, you'll earn 999 all-breed points, but you won't win any breed points (since you didn't defeat any other American Water Spaniels). Rare breeds often travel to other parts of the country to specialty shows or shows that are likely to draw a large number of entrants in their breed to ensure they beat enough members of their own breed to make the cut for Westminster.

- Some breeds are more competitive than others. The fifth-ranking Doberman Pinscher had to defeat 2,166 other Dobermans in 2000 to earn the number-five spot in her breed; a rare Anatolian Shepherd had to beat 26 other Anatolians to rank fifth in his breed.

◆◆◆◆◆◆◆◆◆◆◆◆◆◆◆◆◆◆◆◆◆◆

Chapter 7

The Asphalt Jungle

After a year of planning, dreaming, grooming, and showing, it's finally time. Dogs are loaded into airplanes and everyone converges in one place: New York City.

The first clue that something is really different occurs at the airports: La Guardia, JFK, and Newark are full of dogs. Big dogs in big crates, small dogs in carry-on Sherpa bags, dogs getting into taxis or airport transportation on their way to Manhattan. Even in New York, this scene raises a few eyebrows.

The drive into the city is breathtaking. Like other tourists, dog handlers are impressed by the incredible flow of traffic and the near misses that are part of the daily commute. These folks have their white knuckles clenched firmly to their dogs' crates.

Taxi drivers are remarkably aware of the dog show. "I just had a Komondor in my last fare," says one cabbie. "That dog was bee-ute-tee-ful. Just bee-ute-tee-ful." Dog-show people respond with dog-show talk. "My dog is the number-four Silky, and the top-owner-handled dog," says one proud owner-handler. The driver nods as though he understands perfectly.

THE HOTEL PENNSYLVANIA: FROM THE BIG BANDS TO THE BIG DOGS

The destination for most of the doggie set is Manhattan's Hotel Pennsylvania, directly across the street from Madison Square Garden. You can't miss the hotel: There's a giant, inflatable dog on the marquee. The two-story-tall dog is black with pink spots and is the logo for the Iam's dog food company.

Fifty-one weeks a year, dogs aren't welcome at the Hotel Pennsylvania (except as service dogs for disabled guests). During Westminster week, all that changes. The hotel becomes dog central.

The Hotel Pennsylvania is one of New York's grand old hotels. It is currently in the process of a $45 million renovation to restore its one-time glory. When the hotel opened in 1919, it was the largest in the world. Glenn Miller's 1938 hit song *Pennsylvania 6-5000* was dedicated to the Hotel Pennsylvania—which still has the phone number 736-5000. The hotel lobby has been brought back to its former splendor, with gleaming floors and shining chandeliers.

But you can't even see the floor on the weekend before Westminster. All you see are dogs. Hairy dogs, hairless dogs, short-haired dogs, and wire-haired dogs. Dogs in their owners' arms and dogs in crates, sometimes piled four high.

There are booths for half a dozen dog-related companies set up in the middle of the lobby, where the doggie crowd lingers as they greet old friends with shouts and hugs.

Checking into a hotel with a show dog isn't the same as checking in with your family pet. Show dogs come with serious luggage. First of all, every dog has a crate. For the giant breeds, these portable plastic "dens" are the size of an average cave. Lots of the exhibitors arrive with several dogs, so these crates are placed on wheeled carts and then stacked one on top of the other.

Then there are the dog's accessories. Grooming equipment—including hairdryers, foldable tables, chamois towels, and an incredible array of scissors and combs—all comes with the dog. Many exhibitors bring food and water from home so their dog's tummy doesn't get upset. A 100-pound dog can easily come with 200 pounds of paraphernalia.

Not every Westminster competitor is a Rockefeller, not by a long shot. Often competitors will crowd four or five to a tiny room, then add a half dozen dogs and their equipment.

The hotel staff takes it all in stride. "It's a lot better than when the Grateful Dead stayed here," says Steve Leonard, the energetic Director of Sales and Marketing for the hotel. "Besides, these aren't just any dogs. These are pedigreed dogs." Leonard says that the dogs are remarkably well-behaved—better than some conventioneers who come to town. "This show isn't just *a* dog show, it's *the* dog show," he points out. "It's like the Masters, the World Series, or the Super Bowl. These people are professionals."

Leonard says that the biggest problems they have are with guests who don't register properly. "Someone will take the red eye in from California and arrive here at eight in the morning. They want to get right into their room. But we're full this time of year, and sometimes we can't get them into a room until the regular check-in time. Mostly, when guests are in this situation, we can store their luggage so they can go to Macy's or see a movie. But you can't do that when you have a bunch of dogs with you."

When someone else gets checked in faster, irritable exhibitors have been known to ask, "Are you giving them better treatment because they have a Poodle and I have a Pug?"

The hotel gears up for Westminster like an army going to battle. They set aside 900 out of 1,700 rooms for the show. They plan for extra housekeeping staff, extra bellhops, and plenty of extra towels and bedding. They pray that the hot water holds out, given the demands of a full house, along with many, many dogs. The sidewalks and sides of the hotel are regularly pressure-washed to keep them fresh and tidy.

"The show has a big effect on our lives," says Nancy Veit, Guest Services Manager. "It's lots of extra work."

The hotel creates "exercise runs" on each floor so that dogs have an indoor spot to potty. These runs are located in the service areas,

providing an enclosed space covered with wood chips so dogs can relieve themselves without going outside.

Lots of dogs—and their owners—are grateful for these exercise
runs. Willie, an English Toy Spaniel, was one of them. When Willie
(Ch. Eli-Fran's Sir William) isn't with his family in Moline, Illinois, he
lives with his handler on a 95-acre spread. "We call him Farm Dog
Willie," says owner Karen Pouder with a laugh. "Willie wasn't about
to pee on the sidewalk." Once they found the exercise areas, Willie
was a much happier camper. "Sometimes you have to wait half an
hour for the elevator," says Pouder.

Despite cleaning up the exercise area and all the other demands
that a thousand dogs add to the hotel's workload, most of the staff says
that Westminster week is their favorite time of year. "These are a nice
caliber of people. They're kind and gentle and pleasant to be with,"
says Veit. "And it's fun to see the dogs. They bring out the kid in us."

Geraldine Fasolino's job may be the one most affected by the
dogs—she's the Director of Housekeeping for the hotel. It's her staff
that needs to be sure dog-lovers and other guests have clean rooms
and pleasant hallways. She says the extra work is worth it. "People are
so happy to be here. And each dog is more gorgeous than the next. I
brought my 4-year-old daughter here after work just so she could see
the beautiful dogs. The owners let her pet them. She had a wonderful
time."

Culture Shock

People come from all over the world to compete at Westminster. So
when the English accents of the couple eating breakfast at the next
table drifted over, it was natural to ask, "Did you come from Great
Britain just to see the Westminster dog show?"

They exchanged a look and, then howled with laughter. The
woman spit out her coffee as she exclaimed, "So that's what's going
on!"

The couple had just come to New York for their first vacation in the United States and happened to pick the Hotel Pennsylvania during Westminster. They admitted that they were stunned by the array of dogs coming in and out of the hotel. But they just chalked it up to crazy Americans who all seem to have a "thing" for dogs. Happily, they were dog lovers and added an excursion to the dog show across the street as part of their American adventure.

This couple weren't the only ones surprised by what they saw when they checked into their rooms. New York's Hotel Pennsylvania has 1,700 rooms, and 800 of these rooms are filled with people who aren't in town for Westminster. Hotel staff credits the training of the show dogs for the fact that there are remarkably few conflicts. "We might have a hundred dogs in the lobby," says Guest Services Manager Nancy Veit, "and not a single dog will be barking."

A Crisis of Bichon Proportions

Most of the top dogs are staying at the Hotel Pennsylvania. Fanny the Bloodhound is there with her handlers, Bruce and Gretchen Schultz. J.R. the Bichon is also there.

"The cleaning lady loved J.R. She was really nice to us," says Scott Sommer. But there was a catastrophe that could have ruined everything. "The first room we were in had blue carpeting," says Sommer. At one point, he looked down—and J.R. was a blue dog. Tiny bits of carpet lint had worked their way into J.R.'s white coat. "It took four days of daily grooming to get out all the blue fuzz," says Sommer.

And it's hard to be patient when your heart is pounding. "It's an agonizing week," says Sommer. "You try not to go crazy, not let every little thing bother you. You put so much pressure on yourself to win."

No matter how much pressure you feel, no matter how tense you may be, the dogs come first. Sometimes the best thing for you both is to take a nice walk. Except that you're smack dab in the middle of Manhattan.

THE DOGS TAKE MANHATTAN

Manhattan has to be the goofiest place on earth to hold a dog show. This place is all asphalt and concrete and skyscrapers. There isn't even a garden at Madison Square Garden.

Great rivers of people flow from the subway stop near The Garden to the monumental high-rise office buildings, and then flow back into the maw of the subway. New Yorkers walk as fast as most people run, holding their cigarettes out from their bodies as they weave through the crowds. It's hard to imagine enough room for a Chihuahua to slink through these sidewalks.

The noise is like no other place in America. Doormen's whistles blast shrilly, calling for taxis. Traffic is mired in perpetual gridlock while horns honk incessantly, as if that would make things move faster. People speak in shouts. It's an intimidating sight for those who are used to the pace of small towns—and even of other large cities.

Surprisingly, most of the dogs take the scene in stride. Not only that, but they take over Manhattan.

During Westminster week, the streets are full of show dogs. You wouldn't think that 2,500 dogs would have a big impact on a city of 7.5 million people, but they do, probably because almost all of these dogs stay in a handful of hotels within a couple of blocks of Madison Square Garden. Go for a stroll on the Sunday night before Westminster begins, and you'll see scores of show dogs out for one final pee prior to bedtime.

Many of these dogs wear outfits. No, they're not sporting cute little sweaters. These dogs wear serious gear. Their carefully groomed and bathed fur has to be protected from the gritty city air. Lots of dogs wear little booties slipped over their paws to protect their feet from broken glass and street grime. A few sport the popular K-9 Top Coat, a lycra bodysuit for dogs. This canine fashion frock covers a dog's entire body from neck to ankles in four-way stretch fabric (available in a variety of fashion colors and prints), so the dog can enjoy an outing without damaging his fragile coat.

The Poodle

Sometimes it's the show dogs who stun the New Yorkers, rather than the other way around.

A Standard Poodle in show coat is an amazing sight. A Standard Poodle is a good-sized dog, standing nose to nose with a Labrador or a Collie. A show cut gives these dogs a huge, fuzzy blanket of hair that stands straight out from their chest and neck. Pompons are carefully sculpted on hip and knee joints. And their back ends are shaved down to the skin.

As unusual as a show trim looks in the ring, it's nothing compared to how bizarre a Poodle looks between shows. Handlers carefully wrap the precious hair of the dog's topknot in blue plastic to preserve the coiffure around the Poodle's face. Picture a head full of dreadlocks, carefully preserved lock by lock in shiny plastic. Show Poodles wear long leggings when they're out on a walk to ensure that those perfect pompons don't become sullied by the dirt on the street.

Right beside the front entrance to the Hotel Pennsylvania, the three street toughs looked like they had seen it all. Nothing was going to faze these guys as they swaggered toward a local bar, apparently looking for some action.

Until they saw the white Standard Poodle being taken out for a pee. The dog's handler was meticulously dressed in pressed blue jeans and a brightly colored jacket. The Poodle was in full regalia, his hair wrapped in blue plastic, jockeying around his leggings as he carefully peed against the side of the hotel.

The three guys stopped in their tracks. "Oh man," said one. "Oh man," replied the other. "Oh man," they repeated in unison. Apparently, they had no other words to describe what they saw.

They then stood in silence, watching in awe until the Poodle and his handler turned and walked gracefully down the street.

Twenty-Five Hundred Dogs in Search of a Tree

When you think of dogs, you naturally think of trees. But unless you're willing to make the considerable hike to Central Park, there isn't a tree in sight. Not a shrub, not a potted plant. The streets of Manhattan really are an asphalt jungle.

Not every dog is willing to use the side of a skyscraper as a substitute for a tree. Some of these dogs need the real thing. They are used to large spaces and aren't amused by the Manhattan landscape.

Arlene Cohen's Field Spaniel, Henry (Ch. Marshfield's Boys' Night Out), is accustomed to the wide-open spaces of Oregon. Arlene was relieved when she found a small, safe park to take Henry for a walk. "I took Henry there and this man starts yelling at me, saying there are no dogs allowed," says Cohen. "I couldn't believe it. Grass and trees, and you can't take your dog there? They let us bring Henry into Starbucks and the Chinese take-out place, but he wasn't allowed in the park."

Forget the Fodor's Guide

On the weekend before Westminster, exhibitors check out New York's tourist attractions. Most dog people don't bother to buy a guidebook to New York City. They have everything they need in a handy little map that's a pullout from the February *AKC Gazette* magazine. This map shows all the main attractions: AKC headquarters, Madison Square Garden, veterinary clinics, dog-friendly hotels, pet shops, dog art galleries, and stores such as Tiffany's that welcome four-legged customers. The map doesn't mention trivial sites such as the Empire State Building or the Statue of Liberty. During Westminster week, you can expect to see dogs in their lycra outfits gazing at the windows of Macy's, or going on carriage rides in Central Park.

Junior handlers receive a lesson they won't learn in school. Most troop dutifully to the Empire State Building and other historic sites with their parents. But they also get to see other slices of life. "I loved the city," says Eva Dawson, who has exhibited as a junior handler for three years. "Mom took us to First Avenue, where they sell the fake Rolexes." Her sister Jennifer, who at the tender age of 13 has been to Westminster twice, agrees that hanging out with people selling counterfeit watches was a lot of fun. She does point out that their mother took them to the Statue of Liberty and other important places. But then she adds, "The best part was shopping. I got a jacket and a skirt."

Signing Books at America's Most Amazing Doggie Daycare Center

The week before Westminster, native New Yorkers and people in town for the show look for activities that revolve around dogs. Writer Janine Adams spent the Wednesday night before the show holding a signing for her book *You Can Talk to Your Animals: Animal Communicators Tell You How,* at Biscuits and Bath Doggy Village in Manhattan. Doggy Village is a five-story canine daycare center with Astroturf play areas, an aquatic center and a human coffee shop. Devoted doggie daycare customers spare no expense for their four-footed "kids." Adams's book is about animal communicators, and she brought a communicator along with her to do most of the talking. Dogs and humans alike ate it up—and snatched up a stack of Adams's books while they were there.

Picture This: Dog Art

When most people go on a trip to New York City, they're likely to check out the sophisticated art scene. Dog people do the same thing, but with a twist. They come to see dog art.

Get out of your head that image of a bunch of dogs sitting around a poker table playing cards. Think instead of 19th-century art, and about serious artists who exemplify some of the finest techniques of their day.

The must-see place to be during Westminster is the William Secord Gallery, located on Manhattan's Upper East Side. Once you come, you'll never think of dog art the same way.

The gallery is on the third floor, so be prepared to take the stairs or ride up on a tiny elevator that barely holds two people. It's worth it.

When the door opens, you're transported into another world. Museum-quality artwork from the 19th century covers the walls from floor to ceiling. And every painting or print features a dog. We're not talking about a dog sitting at his master's feet, or a dog peering out from behind a curtain. In these paintings, the dogs are the stars.

The patina of each painting shines softly under the lighting. There's a radiance to good art—you feel it when you're in an art museum seeing the work of the masters. Secord's gallery puts you in this same trance-like state; it feels as though you're spending an afternoon with the canine version of the Mona Lisa. It's impossible to tear your eyes away from paintings that capture the soul of a dog who wagged his tail over 100 years ago.

These paintings are for serious collectors. They carry price tags from $3,000 to $175,000. But don't worry: There's dog art for those with more modest means. Antique prints, dog collars, and other collectibles start at about $300.

Despite the fact that the art is serious, the gallery isn't. "We all love dogs here," says William Secord, an urbane, impeccably dressed man with a friendly demeanor. "It should be fun to buy a dog painting."

Secord will patiently point out the different styles of 19th-century dog art. There's the Purebred Dog Portrait: four legs on the floor, face to the side with the head slightly tipped toward the viewer. "These paintings were done to show how well the dog conformed to the breed standard," explains Secord. Then there's the Pet Portrait: a sweet, sometimes whimsical rendition of someone's beloved family friend. Finally, there's the Sporting Dog Portrait: dogs hunting, or sometimes resting next to the big pile of fowl that they just retrieved.

Each of these styles of paintings attracts a different set of collectors. Secord says that people who collect dog paintings are great to work with. "People don't buy these paintings because they're an investment, or to show off to their friends. They buy them because they love dogs and they love fine art."

One of the highlights of the year is a special exhibition the weekend before Westminster. "We do a lot of business during Westminster," says Secord. "We even sell (more) paintings to people who live in New York at this time of year, because they're thinking about dogs."

Gilbert Kahn, who owns Joey the Shih Tzu, is a serious dog-art collector. He volunteers his time as chairman of the board of the AKC Museum of the Dog, located in St. Louis, Missouri. Some of Kahn's personal collection is featured in Secord's sumptuous, colorful books about dog painting.

Kahn says collecting dog art has been an interest that's developed along with his interest in dogs. He's bought some paintings from Secord but says he also likes checking out "fancy flea markets" in his travels around the world. "I have dog paintings in my homes—in Florida, New York, and Newport," he says. "It's fun to find them, and figure out who painted them."

The William Secord Gallery is open year-round Monday through Saturday, 10:00 a.m. to 5:00 p.m. (and is open the Sunday before Westminster). To catch a glimpse of this stunning salon, check out **www.dogpainting.com.** Or climb up the three flights of stairs and see it for yourself.

PARTY ANIMALS

Westminster is the annual gathering of the tribe. It's part family reunion, part convention, part trade show, and part Mardi Gras. On the days leading up to the show, everyone's calendar is packed with activities: judges' seminars, a Toy Dog show at the Hotel Pennsylvania, and meetings of various dog-related organizations. Then there are the parties.

There are parties for everything. There's one for Take the Lead, a nonprofit organization that provides financial help to people in the fancy with life-altering health problems. A theater and dinner party benefits the AKC Museum of the Dog. The Westminster Kennel Club honors its judges and members at a black-tie dinner.

On Sunday afternoon, the AKC holds its annual open house. This place is something to see. The walls of the AKC's meeting rooms and individual offices are lined with antique and contemporary dog paintings, bronzes, and all kinds of canine objects d'art. The boardroom looks like any high-powered boardroom in a major corporation, but instead of framed pictures of the firm's founding fathers, the walls are decorated with portraits of dogs.

At all the events, there is an edge. People are talking dogs, and talking about Westminster. Some ask leading questions, hoping to elicit a compliment. "I think we just might have a chance of winning the Working Group, don't you think?" they'll ask. Others steadfastly refuse to even talk about the subject, afraid that whatever they say will jinx them.

The heavyweight parties honor the top-winning dogs. For the past year, everyone in the sport has done their level best to bring their dogs out on top, and it's a big thrill when that achievement is honored. These parties are black tie, and owners and handlers are dressed to the nines. Hill's Science Diet honors the top ten dogs in the all-breed standings—plus other notables, such as the top owner-handled dog, and the Veterinarian of the Year. "It's so classy, so tasteful," says dog writer Mordecai Siegal, who has emceed the event for the past six years. "They give out a Tiffany dish to everyone—and it doesn't even have 'Science Diet' written on it."

Pedigree gives an award for the top-winning dog of each breed. Pictures of the winning dog flash across monitors, and owners cheer when their dogs appear on the screen.

Nature's Recipe pays homage to dogs who have won the most Group wins in each group. In 2001, this event was emceed by dog writer and cable television host Darlene Arden, wearing a fashionable rhinestone pin that says "BITCH."

Best-selling author Amy Tan holds a party at her Soho loft to benefit the Canine Health Foundation. Here, the New York intellectual crowd mingles with the doggie set. Attendees wear slinky black dresses and crisp tuxedos. There are real diamonds and faux—but all of them are large. Tan is clearly a devoted dog lover; her tiny Yorkies, Bubba and Lilli, perch in a designer carrying case so that they can comfortably hang out during the party.

If you like to read about dogs, the Dog Writers Association of America's annual banquet and awards presentation is a slice of heaven.

There are awards for every kind of writing—from canine murder mysteries to newspaper writing to articles in breed-specific magazines. There's no one who reads as much as a writer, and these people are huge fans of each other. "I loved your piece in *Dog World*." "I've been your fan since I was a little girl." "I have your book on my nightstand next to my bed." These people treat each other like rock stars.

The Canine Chronicle and Iam's dog food sponsor what has to be the most festive party of the weekend. This huge bash is held in the ballroom of the Hotel Pennsylvania on Saturday night. Lights in the shape of Manhattan's skyline decorate the ballroom ceiling. Iam's has superimposed their own lights—in the shape of their trademark pink paw prints—on top. It looks for all the world like a pink Pup-zilla is out there somewhere, wreaking havoc upon the city. There are other thematic decorations, such as a dog topiary with a wreath of roses around his neck. Hoards of people—the men in black tie and the women in sequined dresses —dance to rock 'n' roll music and talk about dogs. This event supports a different doggie charity each year—this year it is the Canine Health Foundation. This party raised $13,000 for the foundation; at $10 a person to get in, that means 1,300 people partied underneath those big pink paw prints.

But there is a restlessness at all of these events. A corner of everyone's mind is on the show. Come Sunday night, these people are sure to have more trouble sleeping than a kid on Christmas Eve.

Monday morning finally arrives. It's time to show.

Chapter 8

The Garden

Madison Square Garden sits directly on top of Penn Station—the train, subway, and bus station stop that brings tens of thousands of commuters into Manhattan each day. On Monday morning, as vast waves of people billow out from underground, legions of dogs make their way into The Garden.

Almost none of these dogs is walking. This isn't the time to get their paws dirty on the gritty city sidewalks. Small dogs are carried in their crates. Big dogs have their crates on wheels; their handlers push them through the streets, nimbly weaving through the current of New Yorkers in an apparent dead run toward their offices.

In another city, Madison Square Garden would look huge. But in Manhattan, the arena is dwarfed by the tall skyscrapers surrounding it. The Garden's gray concrete exterior seems unremarkable in the middle of the dramatic city skyline.

Still, The Garden is the world's most famous sports venue. The big pillars in front of the entrance are decorated with giant images of all the great athletes who have performed here. Larger-than-life action shots of tennis stars, basketball players, and wrestlers decorate the gray pillars.

During Westminster, there's a photo display right next to these pillars featuring pictures of the nation's top dogs. Surely, the Bedlington

Terrier depicted in one photograph is as lithe as tennis star Venus Williams. And the giant Saint Bernard must have a better reputation than New York Knicks bad boy Latrell Sprewell. Not to mention that the Doberman Pinscher could probably stare down wrestler Stone Cold Steve Austin any day.

People line up at The Garden's front entrance for their chance to see the most celebrated show in dogdom. They're paying top dollar, too. It costs $40 for an all-day pass ($60 to see the show both days), and you'll hand over $95 for reserved seating. Two-day attendance will top 25,000 people.

While the regular folks come in through the front door on Seventh Avenue, the dogs and their handlers enter via a side door on Thirty-third Street. Handlers and their assistants push, pull, and shove crates, grooming supplies, clothes for the ring, and good-luck charms up the ramp and into the building.

And just when you think that a dog show is the weirdest possible activity to take place in the middle of Manhattan, a guy who works at The Garden says, "This is a lot easier than the horse show in November." He probably has a point.

INSIDE AMERICA'S MOST CROWDED DOG SHOW

If you come to the show at 7:00 in the morning, The Garden is eerily quiet. The signature green carpets cover the floor. There's hardly a dog in the place. Seeing the empty arena is sort of like seeing a movie star in person—and realizing he's a lot shorter than you imagined. The Garden is really just a large basketball arena. There are a lot of seats, but the actual floor space is incredibly dinky.

At Westminster, at any given time during the day's judging, there are about 90 dogs on the floor—and a Mastiff or a Saint Bernard takes up about as much room as Shaquille O'Neal. Plus, every dog has a handler on the end of his leash. Throngs of spectators surround each ring.

It's crowded.

THE SHOW BEGINS AND JOEY THE SHIH TZU SWEATS

Half of the dog groups—the Toys, Terriers, Working, and Non-Sporting Groups—show on Monday. The other half—the Sporting, Hound, and Herding Groups, along with the finals in Junior Showmanship and Best in Show—take place on Tuesday.

By 9:00 a.m., most of the dogs who will show on Monday are in the building. The floor is crowded with spectators. "The Star-Spangled Banner" blares from the loudspeakers. The crowd claps and the show begins.

Joey the Shih Tzu is one of the first favorites to go into the breed ring. You'd think winning the breed would be a breeze for the nation's number-two dog—and far and away the top-winning Shih Tzu. Guess again. Favorite dogs lose all the time.

Every handler knows that giants fall at The Garden. In 1997, Kirby the Papillon (Ch. Loteki Supernatural Being) came into Westminster as the favorite to take the whole show. This flashy little dog with butterfly ears came within a hair's breadth of winning Westminster in 1996 when he won the Toy Group; the Best in Show judge that year said if he hadn't selected the Clumber Spaniel, the award would have gone to Kirby.

So in 1997, Kirby's was the name on everyone's lips. Well, everyone's lips except for the breed judge. When she pointed her finger at the Best of Breed Papillon, she was looking at Ch. Loteki Good Time Charlie. Kirby went on to win Best in Show in 1999, but in 1997 he was out of the running by Monday morning.

"After that day, nothing will faze me in dog shows," says Kirby's owner and handler, John Oulton.

Joey's handler, Luke Ehricht, would rather not learn how he'd react to such a defeat. Ehricht's in the ring with nine other Shih Tzu, and he's doing everything he can to make sure Joey gets the nod. He grooms the dog with a brush, making sure every hair is in place. He baits him with his favorite treat, keeping Joey happy and attentive.

Joey looks good. His cream-and-taffy colored coat sparkles. His gait is strong and sure. His eyes shine with the joy of just hanging out at a dog show with his handler.

Judging the Shih Tzu takes about 30 minutes. But when you're scared you won't win, it can feel like hours. The little dogs are lifted onto a table draped in a purple and gold cloth and carefully examined by the judge, Dr. Robert J. Berndt. Berndt deliberately runs his hands all over each dog, checking for the way that muscle and bone feel under all that hair. Each dog is then marched up and down the ring. Finally, all the dogs circle the tiny, crowded ring together.

Joey's handler doesn't look like he's taken a breath the entire time. You can see the perspiration on his face.

The Garden is filled with thousands of people. Hundreds crowd around the Shih Tzu ring, and dozens of binoculars all over The Garden are trained on Joey. But the opinion of only one person matters at this moment—and that's the judge who's standing in the Shih Tzu ring.

He's made up his mind. He points to Joey.

Luke Ehricht lets out a sigh that you can hear ten feet away. Ehrich can finally breathe. He scoops up Joey into his arms, kissing the dog over and over. The team proceeds to group competition.

Not every top-ranked dog will be so lucky. Before the show is over, there will be some major upsets.

ENJOYING THE DOGS

While the serious show people focus their binoculars on Joey, thousands of other people are just having a good time. The comments you overhear at Westminster can be hilarious.

"These dogs sure aren't like ours," says a man in a serious voice. "That's right," answers his companion, "These dogs are trained."

Another man and his friend look at the Bull Terriers. Recalling the old Budweiser mascot, one man says to the other, "Hey look, it's Spuds MacKenzie." His friend replies, "I think Spuds is still at the Betty Ford Center."

Pat Mitchell and her best friend, Liz D'Onofrio, have traveled from Bucks County, Pennsylvania. Pat wrinkles her nose, and says, "This place always smells like stale beer." But this is the fourth year these friends have come to Westminster—for a girls trip away from their families—and for the joy of seeing all the dogs. "Our friends always ask us if we're going to see a show while we're in New York City," says Pat. "And I tell them we *are* at a show. It might not be Broadway, but Westminster is a great show."

TINY RINGS

While the spectators have fun watching the dogs, the exhibitors worry about the size of the rings. If you watch Westminster on television, you will see a huge ring covered in elegant green carpeting. The judge takes a long look at each dog's gait, and the television commentators will tell you just how important it is for the judge to look at the movement and structure of each dog.

What they don't tell you on television is that the big, spacious ring you see for the group judging is divided into eight tiny rings on Monday (six rings on Tuesday). These rings are probably smaller than the average living room.

All 158 breeds and varieties are judged in these tiny rings. And it can be difficult to evaluate the movement of an athletic little dog, like a Cocker Spaniel, or even a tiny but leggy Italian Greyhound in such a small space. If you have a large, active breed—say a German Short-haired Pointer or a Bearded Collie (a shaggy Herding dog that's know for its springy, athletic stride)—your dog will never be able to really show how well he can move.

"It puts the judge in a quandary," says one long-time exhibitor. "The dog who shows the best in a small ring often has an incorrect, mincing gait. And a dog with a lot of reach and drive will look clumsy because he can't hit his stride." This exhibitor confided that Westminster breed judges are likely to give the nod to a dog they've judged at another show, where they have really seen how the dog moves.

"If the judge gives the breed to a dog that doesn't move well, that judge is going to feel like a fool when the dog is in the group and he can't move."

THE KERRY BLUE: A DOG THAT LIKES TO MOVE

The small rings have to be on Bill McFadden's mind when he brings Mick, the Kerry Blue Terrier, into the ring. This dog likes to move—he covers ground like a racehorse. Even through he's not a big dog, Mick won't look his best in this confined space.

Mick isn't the easiest dog at the show to handle. He was imported from England only seven months earlier, and dogs are shown very differently in Britain. At American dog shows the animals are expected to stand still, their front legs squarely underneath them, their back legs stretched out behind. Experienced dogs are expected to hold that *stack*, all facing in a counterclockwise circle, while the judge weighs the faults and virtues of competing dogs.

Mick wants none of it. He's used to the show style in Britain, where dogs are more animated and no one cares whether the dog faces clockwise or counterclockwise.

Handling this spirited Terrier is something like handling a small stallion. McFadden is one of the best in the business, and he works hard to keep the Terrier focused without taking away any of the joy and fire that make the dog great.

Mick's aura is apparent even among the nation's other top-winning Kerry Blues. From clear across the building, you can see which one is Mick—there's a subtle light that emanates from this dog. Mick doesn't have the chance to move full stride in the small ring, and he is antsy. Still, when it's all over, Mick gets the nod for Best of Breed.

Mick has taken the first step toward a dream: the incredible feat of winning both Crufts and Westminster. Crufts, the English counterpoint to Westminster, boasts entries of about 21,000 dogs. To be the best of the best in England—and then do it in America—has only been done once before. That winning dog was Ch. Stingray of Derryabah, a Lakeland Terrier who won Crufts in 1967 and Westminster in 1968.

Will Mick be the second?

The Strange Saga of Another Kerry Blue

Mick was imported from England in the hopes of winning Westminster. Two decades ago, another Kerry Blue Terrier was sent from the United States to England with the hope of winning Crufts. It's a strange story that changed the history of the breed—and has a lot to do with Mick standing in the ring at Westminster in 2001.

Bernice Kusch was breeding top-quality Kerry Blue Terriers when she was only in her twenties. Her dog, Ch. Callaghan of Leander was doing well, and Kusch was persuaded to allow the dog to go to England. "Callaghan's handler said he could win Crufts," she says. And the handler was right: Callaghan won Crufts in 1979. But the celebration soon ended for Kusch: She couldn't get her dog back. When his handler took Callaghan to Britain, Kusch's name wasn't included on the dog's English registration papers. Kusch had lost control of the dog she loved. Entreaties for help—even a trip to England—didn't do any good.

In the United States, Callaghan hadn't been bred much because a relative had a genetic disease. Kusch feared Callaghan might be a carrier. The dog's English handler did a test breeding and found out that Callaghan was apparently clear of the disease—and so he bred the dog to a number of Kerry Blue bitches. Callaghan became an important sire in England—and one of his descendents is none other than Ch. Torum's Scarf Michael, the only other Kerry Blue to ever win Crufts.

Kusch says that Callaghan died in South Africa, where he was taken by his handler. But Callaghan's genes live on in Mick, a dog who may just be the most spectacular Kerry Blue Terrier of all time.

A Westminster Best in Show is a real possibility for Mick—if he can make it though the Terrier Group. In the group, a lamb-like Bedlington Terrier will defend his Group First placement. That dog will be handled by Taffe McFadden—the wife of Bill McFadden, Mick's handler.

BENCH PRESSING

Westminster is one of a handful of "benched" shows left in America. At most shows, dogs can arrive just before they're shown and leave as soon as the judging for their breed is over. If you show at 9:00 in the morning, your dog may leave before 9:30.

Westminster is different. Every dog judged that day has to stay in his assigned spot from 11:00 a.m. to 8:00 p.m.—no exceptions.

The benching area is in a large, open room located underneath the floor of The Garden. It's more packed with people than the subway during rush hour. If you aren't a New Yorker, it's likely you've never been someplace so crowded. Think of the worst mall at Christmastime. Then think of it ten times more crowded. Now add over a thousand dogs, and you will have the Westminster benching area.

The mob is so tight that you literally can't breathe. People grab at the dogs they want to pet. Frustrated exhibitors try to get their dogs to the ring. You can carry a Pomeranian over your head and above the crowd—but you just have to hope for the best as you try to find room for a Great Dane.

The "benches" are wooden platforms that are about a foot off the ground; each dog is separated from the next by a wooden partition. While most dogs of the same breed are benched together, professional handlers with several dogs have separate benching areas in a far corner where it's more difficult for the vast crowds of onlookers to find them.

Placed periodically throughout the benching area are odiferous *exercise areas,* small spaces covered with wood chips where dogs can potty.

Show vendors hawking magazine subscriptions, leashes, doggie fashions, and show memorabilia are crammed along the walls.

This isn't the place for the claustrophobic.

1998 was the worst year ever. There was a conflict between the show's regular date and a basketball tournament, so Westminster was bumped to February 16 and 17. No one realized that President's Day fell on February 16 that year.

With New Yorkers and their kids looking for a fun, holiday activity, the show was swamped. "It was terrible," remembers dog writer Janine Adams. "By mid-day, the Fire Department had closed down access to the benching area."

Exhibitors were screaming at throngs of spectators who were packed too closely to move aside. Dogs were in danger of losing their shot at Westminster glory because they couldn't get to the ring.

"I remember a woman who was trying to get her Labrador to the ring," says Adams. "Finally, in frustration, she screamed, 'Bitch coming through!' and the crowds parted."

And that wasn't the worst of it. The ventilation in the benching area isn't adequate for all the dogs and all the people in a normal year. It's incredibly hot and stuffy in the best of times. In 1998, it was unbearable.

"It was the worst condition imaginable," says Dr. William Newman, one of the owners of the great Alaskan Malamute Ch. Nanuke's Take No Prisoners, who won the Working Group in 1998. "We got bags of ice and kept him covered with ice. The dogs should come first. The conditions that year were just terrible."

There are always suggestions to move the show to a roomier venue, or to invite fewer dogs. But as usually happens with the Westminster Kennel Club, tradition wins out. For 118 years of the show's 125-year history, it's been held at Madison Square Garden. In the year 2002, the show will once again be held at The Garden. Tradition demands it.

TRADITION!

Understand a little bit about the Westminster Kennel Club, and you'll understand why tradition means so much.

The club is named after the Westminster Hotel, a once-fashionable meeting place for New York's elite and the original gathering place for the members of the club. Those early members were all white and all male—and, presumably, all wealthy.

The Westminster Kennel Club Dog Show has been held every year since 1877. It's the second-oldest continuously held sporting event in the United States after the Kentucky Derby, which began running less than two years earlier. The Westminster dog show has been faithfully held despite two world wars, the Great Depression, several crippling blizzards, changing times, and changing fads.

In 1877, the streets of New York City were full of horse-drawn carriages, not taxis. Currier and Ives prints were very popular at the time; but these beautiful lithographs weren't quaint scenes of a bygone era, they were pictures of contemporary American life.

The Westminster show was organized just 12 years after the end of the Civil War. The "Indian Wars" that pitted the United States government against Native Americans weren't over. Chief Joseph and Geronimo had yet to lay down their arms. It was four years before Billy the Kid's outlaw days ended with a fatal shot. Buffalo Bill Cody was wowing crowds with his Wild West Show starring Chief Sitting Bull and Annie Oakley. (Coincidentally, the Broadway show *Annie Get Your Gun*—about Annie Oakley—was playing to sold-out crowds during the 2001 Westminster Show.) Henry Ford turned 14 years old in 1877. America's national pastime of baseball was still in its infancy; the National League was formed just one year earlier, in 1876.

The American Kennel Club, which sets the rules for purebred dogdom in this country, didn't form until 1884. Compared to the Westminster Kennel Club, the venerable AKC is a mere pup.

Tradition—and history—matters to these guys. You can tell by looking at the show catalog. Every dog show in America has a catalog that's a goldmine of information. It lists all the entries, including the dog's AKC number, the names of the dog's sire and dam, the name of the breeder, and the name and address of the owner.

The Westminster catalog includes all of that—and plenty more. It also lists the name of every Best in Show winner since the award was first made in 1907, along with the name of the owner and the name of the judge. It then tells you who was President of the Westminster Kennel Club that year, and who was the show's chairman.

Holding the show at the prestigious Madison Square Garden is a big deal to show organizers. The distinctive royal purple color that is the hallmark of all Westminster items—including the show catalog—exactly matches the royal purple seats in The Garden. Half of the time, the Westminster show is just called "The Garden." So the truly sophisticated don't say, "My dog made the list to be invited to Westminster." No, they say, "Yes, we're going to The Garden again this year."

The show just wouldn't be the same anywhere else.

No Girls Allowed!

Go to any dog show, and you'll see it's predominantly a woman's sport. Westminster is no exception. Women can—and very much do—participate in the show. Similar to over 1,400 other dogs shows in America (which are organized by local dog clubs), the Westminster Kennel Club follows the rules of the American Kennel Club in its show operations. Entries are open to everyone, of both genders, all races, and every economic circumstance.

In fact, women have handled dogs at the show since the turn of the 20th century; more than half the dogs in 2001 were handled by women. The first woman to judge a dog show anywhere in the United States judged at Westminster in 1888. In the past 20 years, 11 women have been given the club's highest honor—judging Best in Show.

But the Westminster Kennel Club itself—the members who put on the show, who select the judges, who carry on the tradition of the world's most prestigious dog show—is a boys' club, and there are no girls allowed. Just as it was when it was formed in 1877, the members are still all white, all male, and, presumably, all wealthy.

SHOWER, WILLIE, AND THE LITTLE DOGS

At the English Toy Spaniel ring, no one is thinking about the past. All that matters is what's going to happen in the next few minutes.

Jerry Elliott and Shower are ready. But Jerry's nervous. "We showed under this judge before and he liked Shower, but you never know what's going to happen. All of the top five dogs were there."

One of those top five dogs is Willie (Ch. Eli-Fran's Sir William), owned and bred by Karen Pouder and her husband Frank. "We thought Westminster was just for the elite—for rich people," says Karen, a friendly woman from Moline, Illinois. "We're just regular people who show our dogs." The past year the Pouders kept track of the statistics, and by September realized they were ranked number four in the breed—and would be invited to Westminster. "It was incredibly exciting," Pouder says. "We knew people who had gone, but we didn't know anyone who'd actually shown there. We went on the Internet to get advice about what to do and where to stay."

Over the weekend, the Pouders did the whole New York routine: They attended Broadway plays, visited Central Park, even ate at the famous Carnegie Deli. "You can't comprehend the price of things," says Pouder, who'd been to Chicago many times but found New York incomparably larger and more expensive. Still, it was fun. "Now, every time I see something from New York on television, I recognize it," she says.

While Pouder says she found the crowds at Westminster a little overwhelming, Willie took it all in stride. "Willie wasn't the least bit intimidated," she says proudly. He sat happily on the top of his crate in the benching area, greeting people as they came by. "We said to him, 'This is Westminster, you're supposed to be excited.'"

At 1:15, the judging began. English Toy Spaniels are divided into two different varieties by color: the King Charles and Ruby are solid-colored or black and tan dogs; the Blenheim and Prince Charles are parti-colored (white with spots of color). Shower and Willie are both Prince Charles (tri-colored) dogs.

The cuteness of these dogs is undeniable. They've been companions since the Renaissance. "Did you know these dogs were bred to keep the fleas off people? This was in the courts of Europe, but people still had fleas," says Jerry Elliott. He looks down at Shower with a smile. "It's nice to be needed."

The breed's background as companions is evident in the way they show. They look up at their handlers with big, sweet eyes, and wag their tails.

Shower is having the show of her life. "Her performance surprised even me," says Jerry, the excitement evident in his voice. "She was very excited—she loves to hear applause. Shower thinks it's for her, even when it's not," says Jerry.

Shower is moving beautifully, her head up and tail wagging. It is everything that Jerry and John hoped this little dog would do.

Meanwhile, Karen and her husband Frank are thrilled with Willie's performance. They've been baby-sitting their handler's Cocker Spaniels during the last year in exchange for free handling. And now Willie is showing his heart out. "When his feet hit the ring, he said, 'Okay, I like this,'" says Karen. She's up in the stands, trying to take pictures. The guards keep making her move so that she doesn't tie up the crowds.

There are five gorgeous little dogs in the ring. Their adorable, flat faces and luminous eyes look beseechingly at the judge. Their little tails are wagging.

The judge points to Shower for the Best of Variety. It's the second year in a row that's she's won the Variety, and the eighth time one of Jerry and John's dogs has won. Jerry is thrilled and relieved. "You just don't want to lose at Westminster," he says.

Best of Breed or Variety isn't the only award. Each breed also has an award for Best of Opposite Sex (in this case, since Shower is a female, the Best of Opposite Sex would go to a male). The show also gives Awards of Merit for the best remaining dogs in the breed. For this variety of English Toy Spaniel, there was just one precious Award of Merit available.

Karen Prouder holds her breath. Best of Opposite Sex goes to the number-two ranked dog, Ch. Little Artist de Vilfloraine.

Then judge Everett Dean, Jr., makes his Award of Merit choice—and points to Willie. "I don't know how you describe that feeling," says Karen. "Our attitude has always been that we're nobody. We don't have money. But our dog won an Award of Merit at Westminster. We got a really cool medallion, and a cool purple ribbon. He looked wonderful for his young age and maturity level. We were very pleased."

Shower will go on to show in the Toy Group that evening. Karen and Frank Prouder will go home to Moline in a couple of days—and show their friends their award. "My husband doesn't say too much. My husband is Mr. Laid Back," says Karen. But she reported that after they got home, Frank made sure that everyone who came to their house saw the Award of Merit that Willie earned at Westminster.

◆◆◆◆◆◆◆◆◆◆◆◆◆◆◆◆◆◆◆◆◆◆◆

Breeds and Varieties

The American Kennel Club recognizes 158 breeds and varieties. A *variety* is a dog of the same breed, but is different enough in appearance that the breed's parent club and the AKC have agreed that the dogs should be shown separately. For example, rough-coated and smooth-coated Collies; smooth, wire-haired, and long-haired Dachshunds; and Toy, Miniature, and Standard Poodles are all varieties of the same breed. The winner of each variety competes in the Group competition—for example, all three coat varieties of Dachshunds compete in the Hound group. When a dog who competes in a variety wins, it's technically called *Best of Variety*, not *Best of Breed*. (The winning Toy Poodle, for example, is correctly referred to as the *Best of Variety*, but even dog show exhibitors will often use the term *Best of Breed* in regular conversation.)

Over time, it sometimes becomes the practice not to breed dogs of one variety to another, and they become separate breeds. For example, Smooth Fox Terriers and Wire Fox Terriers used to be two varieties of the same breed; eventually, they were recognized as two different breeds.

◆◆◆◆◆◆◆◆◆◆◆◆◆◆◆◆◆◆◆◆◆◆◆

FASHION FAUX PAWS

Every dog at Westminster is painstakingly and meticulously groomed. The same can't always be said of the humans at the show.

Westminster week is also fashion week in Manhattan. The nation's top designers have big-name models strutting their stuff on the runways, giving the press a peek at next fall's fashions. With America's fashion mecca at their doorstep, you'd think a little style would rub off on the doggie set.

Not so.

People who spend hours teasing the topknot on a Shih Tzu often forget to comb their own hair. This is a group that doesn't have a clue that polyester is no longer a fashion fabric.

To be fair, dog fanciers care more about hounds than they do haute couture. The stars of Westminster aren't the humans—they're the four-footed, furry beauties that strut their stuff for adoring crowds. The way to shape a Poodle's pompons, the proper outline of a Bichon Frise's topline, whether or not you trim the whiskers on a Weimaraner—all of these decisions are subject to the whims of fashion. And every serious fancier has an unerring instinct for what is hip and cool in canine styles.

They just don't pay such close attention to human fashions.

Dog people really do dress differently. For example, there are the T-shirts. There isn't a dog fancier around who doesn't have an endless supply of T-shirts depicting her favorite breed. Want a hand-embroidered T-shirt with a Dandie Dinmont Terrier on it? Just check out the vendors at any large dog show. Need a cartoon Boxer, complete with big boxing gloves on his paws? No problem. There are even quasi-abstract, minimalist T-shirts available for people who are tired of all the realistic dog T-shirts they have.

Then there are the general, doggie-themed clothing and accessories. There are knitted sweaters sporting merry Terriers. There are spectator pumps with black and white paw prints decorating the toes. And there is an endless variety of vests—vests with dog designs woven into the fabric, vests with dog photos scanned onto the cloth, or vests with dogs appliqued onto the material.

Make no mistake about it: This stuff is high fashion in canine couture. Wear your Yorkie skirt with your matching Yorkie vest, and you're sure to garner compliments.

At the Fall 2001 Bryant Park fashion shows, the necklines were low and the military look was hot. At the Westminster Kennel Club Dog Show, anything with paw prints on it was in big demand.

In the Ring

Clothing in the ring tends to be pretty conservative. Sport coats and ties for men, dresses for women—perhaps with a subtle pair of 14-karat gold Golden Retriever earrings.

Handlers want to draw attention to their dogs, not to themselves. Well, unless you're Michael Canalizo. For nearly a decade, this handler was identified with Ch. Tryst of Grandeur, a flashy Afghan Hound who mirrored Canalizo's flamboyant attitude and attire. When Tryst won the Hound Group at Westminster in 1996, Canalizo wore a sequined tuxedo jacket into the Best in Show ring.

Occasionally, a young woman will show off her assets as she's showing off the dog's. At one point on the circuit, a woman showing a German Shorthaired Pointer wore a miniskirt that barely covered the basics. And it had a slit up the back. The ring steward looked at the young woman, sighed, and muttered, "That's an outfit you wear when you don't want the judge to look at your dog."

Women have a lot more to consider than fashion when they're searching for the perfect show outfit. Clothes need to be loose enough to run in, but a skirt better not flap in your dog's face. If it does, he won't gait right. Outfits need cavernous pockets since handlers go into the ring with bait (usually cooked liver), combs (have to keep that Pomeranian looking his best every minute), and sometimes even a water bottle to keep the dog cool.

Then there's color. Your clothes are only a backdrop for your dog. If your Irish Setter is set off by your green outfit, wear that. It doesn't matter that you look sallow in green as long as your dog looks his best.

Finally, there's the matter of footwear. It's really bad form to fall on your rear at a show—your dog won't look his best if you're sprawled across the floor. So for most handlers, tennis shoes are the footwear of choice.

At Westminster, black-tie attire is optional in the group rings and expected in the Best in Show ring. Frantic women handlers some-times spend hours across the street from Madison Square Garden at Macy's searching for an evening gown with pockets—one that will look okay with their tennis shoes.

Fur-Bearers

You see a lot of women—and some men—traipsing around West-minster with mink coats. It's hot and stuffy in Madison Square Gar-den during the show, and it's got to be uncomfortable to lug around such a heavy coat. But fur coats are everywhere.

The dog show set—especially the East Coast society set—doesn't share the sense of political correctness about furs that the left-of-center, West Coast, adopt-a-dog-from-a-shelter set epitomizes.

There certainly are people at Westminster who believe that fur is best when it stays with its original, four-footed owner. But at least for now, it's still stylish to wear your mink, sable, or fox to The Garden.

Speaking of Looking Stylish

The grooming area is a big, open space near where the dogs are benched. It's filled with specially-designed grooming tables that handlers bring to the show, along with doggie hairdryers, and boxes and boxes of grooming supplies.

AKC regulations don't allow a dog's appearance to be artificially altered (unlike Miss Universe, who's welcome to use all the silicon she wants to enhance her appearance). But there are always stories of dogs who have been dyed to look the exact, right shade of black. A few years ago there was a Silky Terrier who, the competition claimed, changed from a silver-coated dog to a golden-coated one, depending on the judge's preference. In some cases, only a dog's hairdresser knows the truth. But judges aren't so easily fooled, and changing the appearance of a dog can get the dog and his handler kicked out of competition.

While it's not acceptable to change a dog's appearance, it is imperative to maximize it. And this takes a lot of effort. Handlers and their assistants work on dogs for hours in the morning before they arrive at The Garden. And then the grooming starts in earnest. Dogs are allowed to be away from their benching areas for an hour and a half before show time, and especially with the elaborately coated breeds, handlers use every minute of this time.

A handler and two or three assistants hover over each dog. They rub white chalk onto white fur, then carefully groom out every vestige of powder. They spray to make a Poodle's hair stand up. They tie Shih Tzu, Yorkie, and Maltese topknots with precious bows, selecting colors that will best show off the dogs' coat or eyes. Handlers hold Poodles by the muzzle so they won't mess up their hair. They carry Malteses in the air, like a waiter holds a tray, to make sure that no dirt from the floor smudges their gleaming, white coats.

THE BICHON GOES ON

There isn't a dog at the show who's more perfectly groomed than J.R., the Bichon. You see it when Scott Sommer brings the bouncy dog into the ring. There are 12 fuzzy white dogs with black eyes. But none of the other's coats gleam quite as brightly. A couple of dogs show faint traces of yellow stains around their mouths—but J.R. is just black lips and stunning, white coat.

Scott Sommer seems casual and calm. Someone tells Sommer that one of his assistants did a great job handling a Poodle. A woman leans over the purple railing and asks if this Bichon is J.R., and Sommer chats politely with her for a minute.

Sommer is calm on the outside, but inside, he's wound tight. J.R. might have gone Best in Show at almost half the shows he stepped foot in during the past year—but there was one show where he didn't win Best of Breed. Sommer doesn't want this show to be the second one. "You can always lose," he says. Behind his calm, relaxed demeanor is someone paying very close attention to every other dog in the ring—and to the judge.

When it's over, J.R. and Scott Sommer win the breed. They've got about five hours to eat and to groom J.R. for the Group competition that night.

Tonight will be all about glamour and sequins and television coverage. Millions will watch Joey the Shih Tzu, Shower the English Toy Spaniel, Mick the Kerry Blue Terrier, and J.R. the Bichon. It's what every breeder, what every handler, what every purebred fancier dreams about.

And it's just a heartbeat away.

Chapter 9

Bright Lights and Big Wins

By 8:00 on Monday night, Madison Square Garden has been transformed. It's undergone the kind of metamorphosis that turns a community auditorium into the magical scene of a play, or transforms the school gym into the romantic setting of the school dance. The floor of the arena, which had been crowded with eight tiny rings and mobs of spectators, is now one giant ring. The green carpet shows brightly under the roving spotlights. There are huge arrangements of flowers in the middle of the ring, right next to the little signs that say "1," "2," "3," and "4"—the all-important group placements.

There's a whole new level of excitement and expectation in the air.

The crowd rises as a tape of "The Star-Spangled Banner" is played. An Alaskan Malamute waiting to go in the ring for the Working Group howls plaintively.

It's a fitting way to start the night.

The announcer intones, "Can we have the Working dogs to the ring, please?"

The dogs burst into the arena from behind the press box. The Working breeds are the big boys of dogdom. They're the dogs who pull sleds and guard houses.

◆◆◆◆◆◆◆◆◆◆◆◆◆◆◆◆◆◆◆◆◆◆◆

The Working breeds

Akita, Alaskan Malamute, Anatolian Shepherd Dog, Bernese Mountain Dog, Boxer, Bullmastiff, Doberman Pinscher, Giant Schnauzer, Great Dane, Great Pyrenees, Greater Swiss Mountain Dog, Komondor, Kuvasz, Mastiff, Newfoundland, Portuguese Water Dog, Rottweiler, Saint Bernard, Samoyed, Siberian Husky, and Standard Schnauzer.

◆◆◆◆◆◆◆◆◆◆◆◆◆◆◆◆◆◆◆◆◆◆◆

The press sits at one end of the ring. At the other end, a platform holds USA Network's hosts David Frei and Joe Garagiola. To one side, there's VIP seating for members of the Westminster Kennel Club, their wives, and judges. Everyone in the VIP section is dressed to the nines, in tuxedos and sequins and hairdos and diamonds.

The dogs stand in front of boxes in the Westminster royal purple and gold colors. Each box has a breed name on it. These big, square boxes are clearly visible to The Garden's audience, and they also show up well on TV. So when the you see a big, shaggy, black, tan, and white dog with a sweet face, you can read that he's a Bernese Mountain Dog.

These boxes also have a second purpose. Handlers store all the things a dog needs in them. They stash spray bottles of water—show dogs know how to properly drink from the little nozzles so their faces don't get wet. Handlers of drooling breeds such as Newfoundlands and Bullmastiffs, store big cloths in their boxes. And there's always extra bait, combs, brushes, and squeaky toys.

The Working Group judge is Dr. Klaus Anselm, a slim, serious, gray-haired man who grew up in Germany. He examines each dog in the alphabetical lineup and tells the handler to gait the dog down the ring and then back to him. Anselm looks to see how well each dog conforms to his breed standard—and how well built he is to do the job he was bred to do.

In 1998, the Alaskan Malamute Ch. Nanuke's Take No Prisoners won the Working Group. When owner Dr. William Newman thanked judge Barbara Heller for giving the dog the group, she answered, "I didn't *give* him the group. He's the most beautiful Malamute I've ever seen. I feel as if he could pull me all night long through the snow." Klaus is looking for that kind of quality—a sled dog who can travel through snow, a guard dog with the athleticism and keenness to know the difference between friend and foe.

The number-one Working dog coming into Westminster is Ch. Storybooks Rip It Up, a flashy brindle and white boxer with a black mask. This dog is also the fifth-ranked dog in the country. The Saint Bernard, Ch. Trusts Gentle Ben V Slaton, is the sentimental favorite— he's owner-handled by an auto mechanic from Ohio—and is ranked as the number-two Working dog and is sixth on the all-breed list.

The Doberman entry is the candidate for the dog with the best name. He's Ch. Marienburg's Repo Man—son of a dog named Lex Luthor. Who'd want to mess with a Repo Man who's the offspring of the only villain that Superman really feared? Plus, this dog beat last year's Working Group winner in the breed ring, and he's the number-four-ranked Working dog in the country.

The crowd at Westminster isn't shy. Every time a dog moves, every time a camera picks up a great shot of a dog and shows it on the overhead monitor, the crowd claps and whoops and hollers. The favorites receive big cheers. It feels more like a Knicks game than a typical dog show.

After half the dogs have been gaited, a red light goes on at the judge's table. It's time for a commercial on the USA Network. Anselm sits down until the green light goes back on, and then he's up on his feet, repeating the process for the second half of the group.

Anselm relaxes during another commercial break. When the green light goes back on he makes the cut.

The cut is a big deal. This is the selection of dogs that he's seriously considering for placement in the Group. It's when a handler's heart really pounds and she knows her dog is just a whisper away from the biggest win of her life.

Anselm asks the Akita, the musically inclined Alaskan Malamute, the Boxer, the black Giant Schnauzer, the Kuvasz (a large, white, Hungarian, livestock-guarding breed), and the Standard Schnauzer to line up in the middle of the ring.

For the rest of the dogs, it's over. It's something of a shock not to see the Saint Bernard or the Doberman make the cut—but all the dogs in the cut are among the top-ranked dogs in their breed. The other dogs and handlers stand behind their signs quietly to see which one of the remaining six dogs will get the chance to compete for Best in Show.

Anselm is quick and efficient. He tells the Standard Schnauzer to go to the front of the line, tells the Boxer to stand behind him, then the Giant Schnauzer, and then the Kuvasz.

"One! Two! Three! Four!" he says.

The crowd roars its approval. The handlers rush up to hug and kiss Brenda Combs, a handsome woman wearing a red suit that starkly contrasts with the Standard Schnauzer's salt-and-pepper coat. Ch. Charisma Jail House Rock is a handsome, sturdy, business-like dog—and he'll be in the Best in Show lineup on Tuesday night.

The handler of the winning Schnauzer is jubilant. The Boxer team is gracious, but you can see the trace of disappointment on the handler's face. As the dogs leave the ring, the press swarms around the winner. The Schnauzer gets his official photograph taken with the handler and the judge while the press snaps its own shots and calls out questions.

DAHU: A SPIRIT OF WESTMINSTER

The Standard Schnauzer was a bit of a long shot when he won the group. He went into the show as the third-ranked Working dog, but Schnauzers aren't as naturally flashy as Boxers or Dobermans. In the last 24 years, Boxers have won the group five times, and Dobermans have won it four times—Ch. Charisma Jail House Rock was just the second Standard Schnauzer to earn the honor.

But in 1993, the biggest long-shot of all won the Working Group.

"Dahu comes to Westminster every year," says Pat Turner. She's pointing to the pin that she wears over her heart. The broach is the face of a smiling dog with bedroom eyes who wowed the country in 1993, much to the surprise of the oddsmakers—and even his loving owners.

Dahu (Ch. Lajosmegyi's Dahu Digal) was a Komondor, a spectacular, enormous white dog whose hair hung in long Rastafarian dreadlocks. This dog's hair was formed into 2,774 cords up to 2 feet in length; his coat weighed 19 pounds. Every time Dahu moved, the cords moved in concert with him, like giant tassels bouncing in time to the dog's rhythm. Dahu was so spectacular and joyful that Westminster television coverage sometimes still replays scenes of him the night in 1993 when he won the Working Group. Dahu leaped into the air, then glided across the ring full of vigor, confidence, and exuberance.

No one in his right mind would have believed that Dahu would end up as a star at Westminster.

Pat Turner and Anna Quigley had been breeding top-quality Komondors (technically, the plural of Komondor is *Komondorok*) for 13 years when they bred Dahu's litter in 1986. They knew he was a good-quality puppy but decided to keep a female from the litter and found a home for Dahu with a family in Southern Oregon.

What no one knew when Dahu was placed as a young pup was that he would mature into a dog who was much too clever and strongwilled to make a good family pet for the people who bought him. The situation deteriorated when the family's husband was called out weeks at a time for forest fire-fighting duty, while his wife attended college full-time. Dahu was confined for long hours to a backyard, where he was teased by neighborhood children on their way to school.

Dahu Digal, it turns out, means "loud noise." Unfortunately, the confined dog lived up to his name. When the family made the common mistake of slapping the dog in the face when he barked, Dahu began to snap.

Good breeders always take their dogs back if things don't work out. Anna Quigley brought the dog home and bathed and groomed him, working the huge mats in his coat into cords. Rehabilitating Dahu became a group project for everyone who loved him.

"People say that Komondors are a tough breed," says Pat Turner. "What they don't know is what a soft heart these dogs have." Teaching Dahu to trust people again would take a delicate mixture of love, firmness, consistency, and encouragement.

"We saw how beautiful he was," says Quigley. "But we weren't thinking about showing him or anything else. We just wanted him to be steady."

In the early months, Dahu snapped whenever a stranger's hand came near his head. Slowly, Quigley taught him to trust strangers and respect the people close to him. "We learned that he might always want to bite, but Komondors are smart and Dahu could figure out he wasn't allowed to snap," says Quigley. Dahu stopped snapping, but for a long time he would flinch whenever a hand came near his face. Bit by bit, month by month, and dog show by dog show, Dahu gained confidence and became comfortable with being handled.

"I could tell right away if Dahu liked somebody," says Quigley, who handled the dog in the show ring. For a rare breed, Dahu began doing remarkably well. In fact, he won three all-breed Best in Shows, an uncommon accomplishment for a dog who wasn't shown a lot and didn't fall under the category of glamour breed.

In 1993, Pat and Anna decided to take Dahu to Westminster. The big dog was in his prime. He was temperamentally sound enough to show—and it was time to see how he'd do at the most prestigious show of them all.

"Betty Moore was the breed judge," says Quigley. "I remember when she opened Dahu's mouth and counted every one of his teeth." The dog took it in stride, not even flinching. The award for Best of Breed was his.

Turner and Quigley were thrilled. But there was more—much more—to come.

"I could always tell when he was really on," says Anna. "He'd look up at me with those beautiful eyes, smiling." In the group judging that night, Dahu kept smiling. When he gaited, he jumped in the air and landed neatly, continuing his perfect gait. "I just let him do it," Quigley remembers.

Then Quigley and Dahu were among the handful of dogs that made the cut for final consideration. "I remember judge Irene Bivens was going back and forth between us and a Saint Bernard," says Quigley. "I figured she was deciding between third and fourth place. I kept saying to myself, 'Fourth would be so nice.'"

Bivens reached down, holding Dahu's head to take one last look. This dog—who had been hit in the face, whose wary nature had caused him to snap at strangers—looked up at Bivens with soulful brown eyes and rested his chin on her palms.

"She said, 'Put the Komondor in front!'" says Quigley. She doesn't remember much after that. Winning the group, getting the trophy, being followed by the hoard of photographers . . . it was all a blur.

"At that moment, I didn't remember I had a husband or a grandson or anything. I didn't see the cameras coming at us," says Turner, who made it down to the floor from her place in the stands in record time. She wanted to thank the dog who gave the whole crowd such a thrill.

The next night, Dahu made a great showing in the Best in Show competition, but top honors that year went to the great English Springer Spaniel Ch. Salilyn's Condor. This was no disappointment to Turner and Quigley, who had succeeded beyond their wildest dreams.

These two women became many breeders' heroes. They stood for the quiet, competent, breeder-owner-handlers of obscure breeds that don't always get a close look when they compete with more-glamorous breeds. "When we brought Dahu back to the hotel after the show, everyone in the lobby started clapping," says Quigley.

Pat Turner and Anna Quigley will always cherish that year at Westminster. But winning isn't the only gift that Dahu gave them.

Dahu lived to the ripe old age of 14 and was a great sire in the breed. Most of the top Komondors in the country are his descendents.

Still, it was living with Dahu that taught these dedicated dog people the most. Dahu was a sensitive dog who reacted when he felt threatened or cornered. He needed special care and treatment from his owners in order to cope. "Dahu taught me so much about dogs," says Quigley. "I learned about dogs' decision-making abilities as well as their needs. I learned that I have to hold myself together even when I feel nervous."

So when Turner and Quigley come to Westminster, it's only natural that Dahu's picture is on the lapel pin over Turner's heart. And if the spirit of past dogs lives on in The Garden, then surely one of them is a smiling Komondor with bedroom eyes, whose tassel-like cords fly high in the air as he leaps for joy.

FEISTY TERRIERS AND DOMESTIC HARMONY

As soon as judging for the Working Group is finished, the Terriers enter the ring. These are mostly small dogs with wiry coats that are bred to go underground and seek out foxes, weasels, rats, and other vermin. (Terrier comes from the Latin word *terra,* meaning earth.) The winner of the Terrier Group has gone on to more Best in Shows at Westminster than any other group. Terrier handlers all hope that history will repeat itself.

◆ ◆

The Terrier breeds

Airedale Terrier, American Staffordshire Terrier, Australian Terrier, Bedlington Terrier, Border Terrier, Bull Terrier (Colored variety), Bull Terrier (White variety), Cairn Terrier, Dandie Dinmont Terrier, Smooth Fox Terrier, Wire Fox Terrier, Irish Terrier, Jack Russell Terrier, Kerry Blue Terrier, Lakeland Terrier, Standard Manchester Terrier, Miniature Bull Terrier, Miniature Schnauzer, Norfolk Terrier, Norwich Terrier, Scottish Terrier, Sealyham Terrier, Skye Terrier, Soft Coated Wheaten Terrier, Staffordshire Bull Terrier, Welsh Terrier, and West Highland White Terrier.

◆ ◆

Judge Sandra Goose Allen is a small, elegant woman who looks at home in her sequined gown, her hair arranged in an elaborate chignon at the nape of her neck. Allen's quiet elegance is in contrast to the boisterous Terriers in the ring. She smiles widely and claps as the Terriers run in a circle around the ring.

Terriers are the feistiest dogs at any show. As often as not, handlers in the Terrier ring are as scrappy as their dogs. It takes a lot of dedication to show these high-maintenance dogs with their elaborate grooming and independent attitude.

For the past two years, the nation's number one Terrier was Ch. Willow Wind Tenure. "Ten" is a Bedlington Terrier, a graceful dog who is trimmed to resemble a sleeker, faster version of a lamb. Ten is handled by Taffe McFadden.

This is the dog who's considered to be the main competition to Mick, the Kerry Blue Terrier handled by Bill McFadden, Taffe's husband.

Taffe and Bill McFadden look like the perfect suburban couple. He's tall and lanky, handsome in a boyish way. He looks like the guy who'd be president of the local Jaycees. She appears too young to have three children. In a world where few people have the slightest clue about what clothes look good on humans, Taffe McFadden wears fashionable outfits that show off her slim figure.

A lot of dog folks speculated that Taffe would retire Ten when Bill started showing Mick. This was not to be.

Ten is front and center at Westminster—and it's Taffe's job to make the Terrier ring at Westminster Ten's date with destiny, and to pray that the Kerry Blue comes in second.

Of course, there are 25 other Terriers in the ring with a say in the outcome as well.

The crowd screams its support for the Kerry Blue. There is a feeling that history is in the making. It would be something to see Mick win Westminster just 11 months after he'd won Crufts.

Mick looked great in the Breed ring that morning, but he looks even better in the Group ring. He's got the kind of stamina and energy that make him look better each time he goes in the ring. He's still a handful—Bill McFadden sweats in the heat of the ring and with the effort needed to keep this dog headed in the right direction.

The crowd volume goes on overload for the Jack Russell Terrier. The AKC officially recognized the breed just this past year, and the fancy likes to welcome a new dog to Westminster with shouts and cheers.

In her elegant, thorough way, Sandra Goose Allen examines each dog and watches every dog gait. Then she makes the cut.

The Bedlington, Irish, Jack Russell, Kerry Blue, Norfolk, Norwich, and Welsh Terriers are still in the running.

She gives each one a final look, brings Mick to the front, and then places the Norfolk, Bedlington, and Irish Terriers behind him.

Allen has them circle the ring one last time, and points down the line, "One, two, three, four."

The Kerry Blue wins, and is poised on the brink of history.

REQUIEM FOR THE VOICE OF WESTMINSTER

History is being made at this show, whether or not the Kerry Blue wins. There is a new announcer at Westminster.

As each breed is shown, the announcer tells a little bit about the breed's history and characteristics. For more years than anyone can remember, Roger Caras was the official voice of Westminster. However, Caras was gravely ill during the 2001 show, and asked to be replaced for announcing duties.

If you've watched the Westminster telecast over the years, you can hear Caras's voice ringing in your head. And what a voice! Caras's *basso profundo* rang with the richness and solemnity of a Bloodhound's bay—the breed that Caras bred and loved.

Each year, Caras's voice echoed throughout The Garden and on the Westminster telecast. He intoned information about each breed in a way that seemed both intimate and grand. He would describe the Clumber Spaniel as "sedate, dignified if you will, and just a wee bit dour"—stretching the last word out, pronouncing it "dooooo-er."

He'd even give an occasional, historical upbraiding to some of the breeds, like the French Bulldog. "There can be no serious doubt that the French Bulldog is descended from English Bulldogs," he repeated each year. "Some French fanciers have tried to deny any connection with the English dog. Telling a Frenchman that his breed is a spin-off of an English breed is like touting California wines in Paris."

People who watched the program memorized his words. Part of the ritual in The Garden and in living rooms across America was to mouth the mantra about your breed as Roger Caras spoke the words.

On February 18, just five days after the show, Caras died of a heart attack at the age of 72. Those in the fancy know that Roger Caras was more than just a mellifluous voice. He was a bridge between two worlds that were often at war with each other.

Caras was the President of the American Society for the Prevention of Cruelty to Animals from 1991 until 1999. He was also a member of the Westminster Kennel Club and a delegate to the American Kennel Club. In a political context in which some people believe that you have to choose between love of a purebred dog and rescuing a mixed breed, Roger Caras believed that you could do it all. Every year he would exhort the Westminster audience, "Remember, none of these dogs came from puppymills or pet shops!" Then he'd suggest that everyone go out and get a mixed-breed dog from a shelter to add to their household of purebred dogs.

A man who loved all creatures great and small—and most people, famous or humble—Roger Caras was one of the sport's most endearing and popular personalities.

In 2001, Michael LaFave announced the show, and did a marvelous job. Someday, a new person might earn the moniker "the Voice of Westminster." But no one will ever replace Roger Caras.

Sit. Watch TV. Stay.

While the people who are watching Westminster at The Garden hear the announcer, they don't hear any of the live television coverage. Watch Westminster on television, and you'll see the show through the eyes of television commentators David Frei and Joe Garagiola. They're the perfect Mutt and Jeff (no pun intended).

If you're used to hearing expert commentary from David Frei, it's kind of a letdown to go to your first Westminster—and find yourself left to figure out what you're seeing in silence.

Garagiola is a lovable, former professional baseball player who professes to know absolutely nothing about dogs. Every year, he looks at the furry-faced, Old English Sheepdog and asks, "David, how can that dog see?"

David calmly explains that the dog can, in fact, see—and then tells Garagiola that the shaggy fur on the Old English Sheepdog was a utilitarian coat for the dog's hardy ancestors.

Watching Westminster is addictive, and the ratings prove it. About 10 million viewers sit up, bleary-eyed, waiting to see which dog snags the silver trophy.

Why People Watch

"People like to root for their breed. They'll look at the Golden Retriever on the screen, and relate it to their own dog," says Frei. "They're convinced that if they gave their dog a bath and maybe a little bit of a haircut, he'd look just like the dog on TV."

Others watch to see—and sometimes to laugh at—the collection of odd dogs that parade across the screen. No one goes to the dog park and sees a Chinese Crested Dog—a tiny dog who's basically naked except for tufts of hair on his head, paws, and tail. And you don't often see the clown of the dog world: the Irish Water Spaniel, a big, perpetually grinning, liver-colored dog with a curly coat and a short-haired, rat-like tail. Nor is it every day that you see a Papillon, a pretty little dog with huge ears that looks like a cross between a Collie and a bat.

Garagiola and Frei give you a guided tour of all these breeds.

Garagiola (who really is a smart guy and knows by now that an Old English Sheepdog can see through his fur) guilelessly asks questions that the viewer wants asked, while Frei happily provides us with the answers.

But mostly, people watch Westminster to see which dog is going to win. The lights, the music, the sense of history—all these add to the suspense. However, a lot of the drama comes directly from Frei himself.

The Dog Guy

Frei makes you feel like the ultimate insider. Somehow, he makes you care that the dog on your screen is the number-one Brussels Griffon, or that the Otterhound is an upset winner. You roll your eyes with him when he tells you that a dog in the ring will show only for M&M's or marshmallows.

When he tells you about a dog, you can feel his genuine enthusiasm. "That dog is gorgeous," he gushes. Or "Isn't that dog beautiful?" And sometimes he just says, "Wow!"

You see the show though Frei's eyes. It's like going to a concert with someone who really understands jazz—you hear all the notes and subtleties that you never heard before. He pulls you in right through the television screen.

Frei is an unusual mix: part sports guy, part dog guy. Before his stint as the Westminster commentator, Frei did public relations for ABC's *Monday Night Football* and the Denver Broncos.

But Frei is also a true believer. For 30 years, he's been an Afghan breeder, a judge, and a vocal and respected leader in local kennel clubs and humane organizations. He and his wife, Cherilyn, breed and show Brittanys. He speaks proudly of Cherilyn's work in nursing homes, hospitals, and hospices with their therapy dogs.

So when Frei says he can't wait to see who win Best in Show, he means it. That excitement is infectious.

Changing Lives

Marilu Hanson says watching Westminster on TV changed her life.

"I always had pets. I worked as a veterinary assistant and did dog rescue," says Hanson. Then she watched the 1988 Westminster telecast and was hooked. "That's when I knew I wanted to learn more about showing dogs. That's how I got started."

Just now, Marilu Hanson's dog has won the Terrier Group at the Westminster Kennel Club dog show.

THE LITTLE DOGS COMPETE FOR THE BIG HONORS

The Working Dogs and the Toy Dogs are the yin and yang of the dog world. It's incredible that the massive Mastiff and hulking Saint Bernard belong to the same species as the tiny Yorkshire Terrier and prancy little Pomeranian. Instead of having macho names like Repo Man, these little dogs are more likely to have adorable names—like the Smooth Coat Chihuahua named Ch. Fresa's Willy Marry Me.

♦ ♦ ♦ ♦ ♦ ♦ ♦ ♦ ♦ ♦ ♦ ♦ ♦ ♦ ♦ ♦ ♦ ♦ ♦

The Toy breeds

Affenpinscher, Brussels Griffon, Cavalier King Charles Spaniel, Long Coat Chihuahua, Smooth Coat Chihuahua, Chinese Crested, English Toy Spaniel (Blenheim and Prince Charles variety, and the King Charles and Ruby variety), Havanese, Italian Greyhound, Japanese Chin, Maltese, Toy Manchester Terrier, Miniature Pinscher, Papillon, Pekingese, Pomeranian, Toy Poodle, Pug, Shih Tzu, Silky Terrier, and Yorkshire Terrier.

♦ ♦ ♦ ♦ ♦ ♦ ♦ ♦ ♦ ♦ ♦ ♦ ♦ ♦ ♦ ♦ ♦ ♦ ♦

Rumors swirl at every dog show, and Westminster is no exception. Sometimes there's a grain of truth to the gossip, and sometimes not. The people "in the know" are whispering that the Toy Poodle, Ch. Trebor Shortstop, is definitely going to be placed as Group First, over the favored Shih Tzu, Ch. Charing Cross Ragtime Cowboy. In the next half-hour, they'll find out whether this rumor is true.

The Toys come running into the huge ring with all the verve of much larger dogs—except that it takes a Maltese a lot longer to reach the end of the ring than it does a Bullmastiff. But who needs to run quickly if you were bred to be a companion to a human?

Judge Helen Lee James wears beautifully decorated glittery cuffs on her black dress. To get a better look at the tiny Toy dogs, the crowd watches the huge monitor that hangs from the ceiling, which shows close-up camera shots of the dogs. You can see the sparkling, pretty patterns on the judge's cuffs on the monitor as she examines the little dogs.

There are many public displays of affection in the Toy ring. Professional handler Doug Holloway is a big, burley man who handles a Toy Manchester Terrier. While he's waiting to be judged, he holds the slender dog and kisses her gently.

This is Shower the English Toy Spaniel's second Westminster, and she's having the time of her life in the ring. She grins from long, fluffy ear to long, fluffy ear. Her tail wags frantically as she moves across the ring with strong, sure, strides.

"She had the best show of her life," says Jerry Elliott. There's a special pride that only a breeder-owner-handler feels when his dog does especially well, and Elliott's feeling it tonight.

Joey the Shih Tzu looks perfect. He's immaculately groomed, with every hair in place. His green and gold bow sparkles in the spotlights. After the judge carefully examines Joey, handler Luke Ehricht meticulously brushes every hair back into place. He puts Joey on the ground and the little dog gleefully shakes his whole body. As quickly as he can, Ehricht brushes out the little dog once again, and then moves him back down the ring. The dog is showing like the champion that he is. His gait is huge, like a sporting dog. He's smiling, too, and the dark eyebrows on his perfect face point right down to his bright, dark eyes and Kewpie-doll mouth.

But the Toy Poodle is just as perfect. Ch. Trebor Shortstop (called Dottie) is a little silver dog. When Toy Poodles were first popular, they tended to have short legs and weren't as elegant as the Standards and Miniatures. That's no longer true, and Dottie has an exquisite Poodle type. Dottie's mother (Ch. M V P of Ahs, called "Baseball") won the Toy Group at Westminster in 1995. Maybe 2001 will be her daughter's turn.

Judge Helen Lee James makes her cut. She pulls out Joey the Shih Tzu, Dottie the Toy Poodle, an Affenpinscher—a scruffy, little black dog with a face like a monkey's—the Long Coat Chihuahua, the Pug, and Shower, the English Toy Spaniel.

The judge asks the handlers to take the six dogs around in a small circle so he can have one final look at they way they move. She then puts Joey up in front, followed by the Toy Poodle, the Pug and the Affenpinscher.

"One, two three, four," she says. History is made.

Jerry isn't disappointed. "It's rare for an English Toy Spaniel to make the cut," he says. "I couldn't have asked more of Shower than what she gave me. It was her best show."

Luke hugs and kisses Joey, tousling the dog's precious hair in the process. This is a big win. Not only is Joey the top-winning Toy dog of all time, but he's just won the Toy Group for the second year in a row. This dog will never be forgotten.

Now it's time to start thinking about Best in Show. How much history can Joey make?

BELLIGERENT BOXERS AND LUNCH AT SARDI'S

There's one person in The Garden who is thinking beyond the groups—and even beyond Best in Show.

She's Billie McFadden, and she's in charge of lunch at Sardi's on Wednesday, when the Best in Show dog will be treated to lunch.

Billie McFadden's name is confused all the time with Bill McFadden—the Kerry Blue's handler. "Everyone thinks I'm his mother," says Billie. Although she's glad to claim him, Billie doesn't have much in common with Mick's laid-back, California handler.

Billie McFadden is the picture of refined elegance. She dresses in muted, finely woven fabrics. She's originally from England, and has just a trace of an accent; her voice has the sound of a well-read, well-bred person.

She also has a hilarious, arch sense of humor. McFadden wrote *The New Boxer,* a popular book for both beginning and experienced Boxer lovers. She tells the story of the time someone woke up Bill McFadden at three o'clock in the morning, holding her book and insisting on an autograph. When Bill told her about this late-night mistake, she said in her prim voice, "Why the hell didn't you just sign the book and say you hoped they liked it?"

Billie is a long-time Boxer breeder and a respected Boxer judge. Talk to her for ten minutes, and you also learn that she's a dog lover. She'll tell you about the rescue Boxer that she took in. "I realized that this dog couldn't be placed," she said. "If he wasn't handled just right, he'd bite someone." At first it's hard to imagine this petite woman calming a belligerent Boxer.

Then you realize that she's fearless.

The dog soon trusted McFadden, and did everything she asked of him. She kept him as her own, living side by side with her show dogs. Under Billie's care, this dog became a stable and loving guardian of her home—and a partner in her heart. The rescue Boxer was no longer a dangerous dog.

She uses similar talents with people.

Billie is President of the Dog Fancier's Club; their big event of the year is one day after Westminster, when the winning dog is invited to join the group for lunch.

"The dogs gets his lunch on a big silver platter," says Billie. "Some of the dogs eat so gently and with such good manners. Others just gulp, gulp, gulp." The Springer Spaniel who won in 2000 had exceptionally good manners, she says.

But there's a lot more to the Dog Fanciers luncheon than a photo op with the winning dog. The Group and Best in Show judges come to the lunch and explain why they selected the dogs who won. This is a fascinating glimpse into the thinking of show judges, and they give surprisingly candid comments.

This year, McFadden has to be wondering if the guest of honor will be the Bichon Frise that is just entering the ring for the Non-Sporting Group competition.

J.R.: IS THE TIME JUST RIGHT?

It's close to 10:30 at night, but the Westminster crowd is just warming up. They've been treated to one of the best nights ever at Westminster, with spirited dogs basking in the audience's cheers. Now they want to see just how well J.R. will measure up.

The Non-Sporting Group is a hodge-podge of dogs. In the early days, dog shows were separated into Sporting and Non-Sporting. As the fancy grew and as more breeds were recognized by the AKC, some breeds were separated from the Non-Sporting Group and became groups of their own, such as the Working and Terrier groups. The dogs that remained were breeds whose working roles may have been obscured over the mists of time, or companion dogs that were too big to fit in the Toy Group. Depending on their shape and size, these Non-Working dogs gallop, trot, or waddle into the ring.

◆ ◆ ◆ ◆ ◆ ◆ ◆ ◆ ◆ ◆ ◆ ◆ ◆ ◆ ◆ ◆ ◆ ◆ ◆ ◆

The Non-Sporting dogs

American Eskimo Dog, Bichon Frise, Boston Terrier, Bulldog, Chinese Shar-Pei, Chow Chow, Dalmatian, Finnish Spitz, French Bulldog, Keeshond, Lhasa Apso, Lowchen, Miniature Poodle, Standard Poodle, Schipperke, Shiba Inu, Tibetan Spaniel, and Tibetan Terrier.

◆ ◆ ◆ ◆ ◆ ◆ ◆ ◆ ◆ ◆ ◆ ◆ ◆ ◆ ◆ ◆ ◆ ◆ ◆ ◆

The judge for the Non-Sporting group is John J. Lyons.

J.R. is groomed to perfection, with his sparkling white coat in perfect contrast to Scott Sommer's black suit. The Bichon pulls at the end of his leash, eager to show. He smiles when the judge touches him all over. J.R. is on like a light, and the crowd cheers for him.

When the judge makes the cut, there are six dogs under consideration: a low-slung, push-faced Bulldog; a wrinkle-faced Chinese Shar-Pei; a black Miniature Poodle; an imposing, white Standard Poodle; a perky, black Schipperke; and J.R.

This is J.R.'s night. He is clearly energized by the crowd, pulling forward on his leash, flashing his bright, black eyes, and looking every bit the happy companion dog that a Bichon Frise should be.

The judge says, "Can I have the Bichon?" and puts J.R. at the front of the line followed by the Standard Poodle, the Miniature Poodle, and the Chinese Shar-Pei. They go around in a circle together, and Judge John J. Lyons cries out, "One, two, three, four!" Ch. Special Times Just Right! is living up to the exclamation point at the end of his name.

The day doesn't hold a lot of surprises among the winning dogs. But tomorrow there will be some doozies.

Only one dog will be invited to lunch at Sardi's. The question remains: Which dog will it be?

Party Time!

For the people who have gathered from around the country, and even around the world, the end of the night's show at 11:00 p.m. is the start of a night of partying. Almost everyone feels too energized to go to bed. There are old friends to catch up with and new friends to make. It is time to speculate about who will be tomorrow's top dog—and about the puppies back home who just might be headed toward the ring in the next few years.

The only decision now is just where to go. One photographer looks at the members of the Westminster Kennel Club leaving the VIP section. Many are older men, and many of those men have attractive, decidedly younger-looking wives. "Let's go where the Westminster Kennel Club guys are going—you know, the ones with the third-generation, trophy wives," he suggests.

Tomorrow, the competition will start all over again. The next 24 hours will be filled with revelry, disappointment, laughter, and, for one dog, the biggest honor in dogdom.

♦ ♦

In the comfort of your own home

The USA Network airs the Group and Best in Show judging both days live from 8:00 p.m. to 11:00 PM; the program is usually repeated the next morning. For information about the show, go to **www.usanetwork.com/sports.**

♦ ♦

Chapter 10

The Countdown

Tuesday at The Garden is even more intense and emotional than the previous day. Everyone knows that in exactly 14 hours from the playing of the National Anthem, a new top dog will be crowned.

At times, the tension is excruciating. Westminster may last two days—whereas the Kentucky Derby lasts only two minutes—but no one would think of leaving the dog show in the middle of competition any more than they would leave the Derby after only a half-mile had been run.

There are four dogs remaining after Monday's competition.

A little over half the show's 2,500 dogs competed on the first day. Now it's time for the rest to test their mettle.

THE "PUP"ARAZZI

The media coverage is reaching a fevered pitch. For a sport that receives almost no coverage all year long at 1,400 local dog shows, the doggie paparazzi—the "pup"arazzi, if you will—is overwhelming.

All the networks' morning shows—*Today, Good Morning America, The Early Show*—have done pieces on Westminster. Television commentator David Frei has made an appearance on every one of them. This guy must not sleep.

Frei knows what grabs the attention of people as they drink their morning coffee and eat their toast: dogs. So Frei usually brings with him a pack of dogs who are entered in the show. Many dogs (and humans) have become instant, hometown celebrities after Frei introduced them on national television.

In 2000, one of the stars of *Today* was a Lowchen called Bacchi (Ch. Ashford's Lazim Lezze). Bacchi helped *Today* anchor Katie Couric introduce America to the Lowchen.

Lowchen are shaggy little dogs with effervescent personalities. In the show ring, they're groomed a lot like a Poodle, leaving shaggy hair on their head and chest and shaving their legs, rear end, and tail, while fur cuffs decorate their ankles and a plume of hair tops their tail. A Lowchen in this clip is always a conversation starter.

One of Bacchi's owners remember that, backstage, there was some tension. "They had us wait in another little room instead of in the green room," says Janette Swindler. "There were some models in the green room wearing white wedding dresses, and they didn't want the dogs in the same room with them." Swindler pauses and shrugs her shoulders. "I think they were afraid that the models would be jealous because our dogs were prettier."

It's not just the morning shows that have an unquenchable desire to talk about all things canine during the week of Westminster. The press is everywhere—and it's insatiable. The Hotel Pennsylvania staff patiently talks with a crew from CBS News one hour and gives a tour to a Japanese news team the next.

In The Garden on Tuesday morning, the press is trolling for stories. They muscle their TV cameras through the crowded aisles, searching for an odd-looking dog or one wearing a funny hat. If you've got an usual breed like a Komondor, expect to appear on a dozen television stations across the globe.

Some of these reporters look like they'd rather be covering a basketball game. Others seek out the assignment.

"I ask to come," says Jennifer Madden, a pretty, businesslike blonde reporter for New York's Channel 10 news. "I do a piece called 'Mad About Pets' every week." Madden points out that she also does hard-news features and general assignment reporting.

Madden considers Westminster to be sports reporting. "They call it the Super Bowl of dogs, right?" she asks. "They're canine athletes." When someone questions whether these canine beauties are really athletes, Madden shrugs. "It's kind of like when they don't know where to put cheerleaders in the school yearbook. Do you list cheerleading under 'Sports' or 'Activities'?" she replies.

The weirdest example of the media frenzy is Triumph, the Insult Comic Dog. Triumph is a hand puppet that reports on Westminster for *Late Night with Conan O'Brien*. He's part Rottweiler, part Don Rickles. Mostly, Triumph is sexually attracted to the show's dogs. Although he was kicked out of a previous Westminster, in 2001 the club allowed him to return and do his own brand of reporting, which includes admiring the *Dog Fancy* centerfold dog.

MEANWHILE, AT THE FOXHOUND RING

Madison Square Garden smells slightly of stale beer. This must be left over from Sunday's hockey game, or from countless Knicks games. At Westminster, the alcoholic beverage of choice is champagne with strawberries. Vendors walk up and down the aisles, hawking the stuff.

It's 10:00 in the morning, and the English Foxhounds are called into the ring. Dr. William Newman and his friends settle into their seats hoping that Newman's dog, Virgil (Ch. Whipperinn's Virgil J), will breeze through the breed competition. At Westminster, there are no number-13 armbands. Dog show people are too superstitious. Virgil is number five.

Newman knows that Virgil has a real shot at winning the Hound Group. This graceful, athletic Foxhound has been honored at the Nature's Recipe award dinner on Saturday night as the dog who won the most Hound Group firsts in the past year. In the all-breed standings, he was ranked third in the group, in the same pack as Fanny the Bloodhound and Xena the Coonhound.

Virgil is a gorgeous dog with many good qualities—especially his strong, athletic gait. Hound Group Judge Kent Delaney is a man notoriously focused on structure and movement. As the Foxhound judging begins, things look great.

There are six English Foxhounds in the ring. After examining the dogs and having them gait, the judge points her finger at the Best of Breed dog—and instead of giving the nod to Virgil, the award goes to Ch. Sunup's Sweet Success.

Virgil and his handler walk out of the ring empty-handed. Their day is over before 11:00 in the morning.

The Garden has slain its first giant of the day.

Otterhound Dreams

For every top-ranked dog who's unseated, there's the joyful owner of an underdog who's the surprise Best of Breed winner.

Joellen Gregory's Otterhound, Ch. Scentasia's Iron Man NA NAJ (called Tony) wasn't invited to Westminster; he wasn't even ranked among the top ten Otterhounds in the country. Instead, Tony was one of the lucky dogs whose entry made it in the first hour after entries closed.

What Tony lacks in a top-flight show record, he makes up for in fans. "Joellen works with us at the clinic, and will be starting veterinary school in the fall," says veterinarian Kate An Hunter, who practices at the Carver Lake Veterinary Center in Woodbury, Minnesota. "When we found out that she was going to Westminster, we said, 'We're going with you.'" Hunter, three veterinary technicians, and the office receptionist all flew to New York to cheer on Tony. "We call ourselves his veterinary team *and* his fan club," she says. Joellen's mother is also at The Garden, and her sister flew in from Germany. This dog has serious fans.

Otterhounds are big, athletic dogs with course, tousled fur and an amiable expression.

"We sat ringside and were pretty quiet," says Hunter. Tony showed perfectly. "He had charisma. You could really see him show." They were especially proud of Joellen, who handled the dog herself.

Then it happened. Judge Joan Anselm gave the Best of Breed award to the unranked, owner-handled Otterhound from Minnesota.

Back at the benching area, it dawns on Tony's owner and his fan club that there is more to come. "There was this whole bigger competition," says Hunter. Joellen has to decide if she will handle Tony herself in the Hound Group or hire a professional.

"We told her she had to be in the ring," says Hunter. Once this is settled, there is a fashion crisis. What does a veterinary student wear when she's about to handle her very own Otterhound in the ring—with ten million people watching her on television?

GUARD DOGS AND DOG GUARDS

Back in the benching area, it's more crowded than ever.

The group winners from Monday night have their own special area. Dennis Brown, Scott Sommer's 21-year-old assistant, spends the entire day with J.R., the Bichon. Because of the crowded conditions, you're not allowed to place chairs in the aisles of the benching area, so Dennis sits on the hard, wooden boards of J.R.'s bench. J.R., of course, has comfortable bedding inside his crate. "A lot of people come up and say, 'We're picking you to win,'" says Dennis. "I say, 'There are six other dogs who could win. We're crossing our fingers.'"

Dennis is on full-time guard duty with J.R.

People who don't have full-time assistants often hire uniformed guards to watch their dogs. While the rest of the country buys dogs for protection, at Westminster you buy protection for your dog.

No one is going to leave a dog unattended at Westminster for even a minute. There are always mumbled warnings about extremist organizations that may try to "liberate" the dogs.

There are also whispered worries about competitors doing something nefarious. When a dog gets an upset tummy at the show, half the exhibitors secretly blame their rivals.

The Scary Story of Laund Loyalty

It's easy to dismiss all this worry as just a hint of paranoia from dog lovers until you hear what happened in 1929. That year, the Westminster Best in Show winner was a 9-month old Collie pup who wasn't even a champion yet. (Westminster wasn't restricted to champions until 1992.) The Collie's name was Laund Loyalty of Bellhaven, and the 1929 Westminster show was his first—and last—dog show.

In 1969, a then-teenaged Collie lover named Joan Harrigan wrote to the dog's owner, Florence Ilch, and asked why Loyalty was never shown to a championship.

Harrigan was stunned when she received this reply:

Dear Joan Harrigan —
. . . Regarding the wonderful Loyalty. The *reason* he was never shown again (after his Best in Show) at Westminster was because he was *blinded* by acid thrown in his face after his great win, by a *jealous* person. It was hushed up, but we knew who it was. . . .
Florence Ilch

No one ever saw Loyalty in public again, though he lived on for many years on Ilch's property.

Over the years, Ilch apparently gave conflicting reports, sometimes claiming that the dog was scarred by acid, and other times saying nothing had happened. There are those who speculate that Ilch made up the story so no one would see that her perfect puppy had grown up to be a less than perfect adult. There are others, however, who believe that the acid incident did occur.

Whatever the truth, this story represents the bogey man, the big fear that every exhibitor feels. What if someone wants to hurt your dog? You can't take that chance—not even for a second. So you hire guards. Standing next to Rottweilers, Great Danes, or tiny Chihuahuas, you can often find a Madison Square Garden Security Guard hired for the day.

The big concern really isn't the competitors or animal rights "liberators"; it's the swarm of well-meaning people who want to touch, pet, and kiss the dogs. Some spectators poke at sleeping dogs.

Occasionally, they grab a handful of fur just to find out what it feels like. Sometimes they even bark in a dog's face.

"I feel like I'm in the middle of a giant petting zoo," grumbles one exhibitor.

Paul Richards moonlights as a security guard for The Garden and is watching a Pointer—a brawny hunting dog—on Tuesday.

Richards's regular job? For the last 15 years he's been a corrections officer at the city jail on Rikers Island.

Richards says when he was first told that he was assigned to guard a dog, his response was, "Are you serious?" But he says he figured it was a pretty easy way to earn some extra money. "The dog just sleeps," he says.

Because the burly, uniformed man is standing in front of the Pointer, no one stops to poke at the Pointer.

Does Richards think this is a come-down from his real job as a professional corrections officer? "Naw," he says. "I'm used to watching caged animals."

THERE'S A DOCTOR IN THE HOUSE

While owners and uniformed guards look out for the dogs' safety, Dr. David Hicks watches over their health. Hicks is an on-site veterinarian who works for the Animal Medical Center. He's a youthful, wholesomely handsome man with a Tennessee drawl. "This show is a great way to exhibit purebred dogs, but we don't want them to come to any harm." Hicks says that he's seen very few problems at the show, and there haven't been any seemingly serious illnesses. Westminster has given him time to look at a huge variety of beautiful dogs. "You don't see something like this everyday," he says. "When the crowd goes crazy, these dogs perk up and say, 'Hey, look at me.'"

If something did go wrong, the Animal Medical Center is nearby. This five-story building houses over 80 veterinarians who practice more than 20 specialties. It offers world-class veterinary care. It's the place you'd want to be if something went wrong at Westminster.

Which is exactly what happened in 1989.

From Dream to Nightmare

"We arrived in New York on Thursday night," remembers professional handler Andy Linton. He'd flown in from California with a red and tan Doberman Pinscher named Indy (Ch. Royal Tudor's Wild As The Wind, CD). "I let her out of her crate, and I realized she was bloating."

Bloat. It's possibly the most feared word in dogdom. Bloat causes a dog's stomach to fill with gas and to sometimes twist around inside the animal's body. Within a few hours, a healthy, vital dog can die.

Indy, the dog who was favored to take the whole show, was in a fight for her life. Suddenly, winning didn't matter at all.

"We got her to the Animal Medical Center right away," remembers Linton. Veterinarians quickly put tubes down Indy's throat to relieve the toxic gasses building up in her stomach.

For the next 48 hours, Indy's life hung on the line. "Most dogs with bloat die from stress," says Linton. "Indy was wired up and monitored all weekend."

Throughout the weekend, Linton and owner Susan Korp could only wait—and pray. They decided not to talk publicly until Indy's prognosis was clear. "On Saturday night, we got the Science Diet award. I had to go up and accept the award for the top dog in the country," remembers Korp. "No one knew what was going on. They said to me, 'You don't have to cry.'"

Indy, even more than most show dogs, was an athlete. A conditioned athlete's body can heal itself while the rest of us remain sick in bed. And that's exactly what happened.

"They let me have her back on Sunday," says Linton. "They said it would be okay to show her." A veterinarian stayed by Indy's side at the show to make sure she continued her full recovery.

"Half of New York must have treated her," says Korp. "All these people came by to see her, saying, 'I was her doctor' or 'I was her nurse.' Everyone did a wonderful job. They were awesome."

Could Indy come back from the brink of death and go to the top of dogdom?

"When we went into the Breed ring, I was just so relived she was alive. I had her lie down on the carpet when she wasn't gaiting. I'm not an emotional person, but I was crying while she was lying there," says Linton. "I just kept whispering to her."

Sure enough, the judge gave Indy the nod for Best of Breed. "After we won the breed, I told the judge what had happened. She started crying, too," says Linton.

By that night in the Group ring, the audience had heard the story. "Now everyone was looking at her, to see if she was worthy of winning," says Linton. A roar of approval went up when she went to the front of the line as the winner of the Working Group.

By the time the Best in Show competition came along the next day, it was a frenzy. "Indy was in the newspapers. I had a million reporters following me around," says Linton.

When Linton and Indy came running into the ring, the crowd thundered its applause. The dog looked fit and fabulous. "The doctors had done a miraculous job," says Linton. "There wasn't anything wrong with Indy that night."

The judge agreed. Ch. Royal Tudor's Wild As The Wind CD made history when she won Best in Show.

"Westminster was both my dream come true and my worst nightmare, all rolled into one," says Korp.

Twenty-Five Hundred Stories

Indy's story is one of the most dramatic in Westminster history. But walk through the crowded benching area, and you realize that there's a story for every dog. It might be the puppy who almost died at birth, and then went on to become an iron-willed champion. Or the dog with the wagging tail and the doting owner who is someone's very first champion. Or another dog who is the tenth generation of home-bred champions. Or the pup with the gentle eyes who sat vigil week after week while her owner underwent chemotherapy treatments. Or he's the therapy dog who visits a children's hospital every week—and never fails to make a grievously injured child smile.

The Whimsical Tale of Henry

For Arlene Cohen, Westminster has been nothing but a dream.

When Cohen picked out a sweet, liver-colored Field Spaniel puppy to be her pet, she could never have guessed that three years later Henry (Ch. Marshfield's Boys' Night Out), would be the favorite to win his breed at Westminster.

Fate intervened the day that Cohen dressed Henry in a yarmulke and side curls.

Henry is the second dog Cohen has ever owned. When Cohen's boyfriend was persuading her to move from Manhattan to Oregon, she gave him an ultimatum: "I'll move as long as there's room for a dog," she said.

Henry was a well-bred Field Spaniel puppy who was likely to earn his championship. Arlene mostly showed Henry in the ring herself, and she was thrilled when her pet earned the title of champion. It never occurred to her to show the dog as a special, or to compete at the group and Best in Show level.

Arlene was happily taking obedience classes with her retired champion when the Portland Kennel Club benched show came along in 1998. This show requires dogs to stay in the benching area on the day of judging—and it awards prizes for the best-decorated benches. Because the show is held in December, the benches usually have a Christmas theme.

Cohen decided that the Portland Kennel Club needed a little cultural diversity.

She entered Henry in the show just so she could put him on the bench in a yarmulke and side-curls while playing some Hanukkah music in the background. Cohen had fun visiting with friends and was thrilled when her decorations won a prize. She frankly didn't care much about the dog show. But when an experienced handler asked Cohen if he could take Henry into the ring for her, she said, "Sure."

Henry won fourth place that day in the Sporting Group, and suddenly Cohen realized that he was a top-quality dog who should be shown as a champion.

"Everyone told me to send Henry away to live with a handler," says Cohen. "I knew he'd win more if I did that, but I told them, 'No way!' Henry is my pet."

Cohen, a flight attendant, developed an unusual way to maximize Henry's career while staying with him every day. As an airline employee she flies for free, so Cohen and Henry flew together to shows around the country. Cohen hires a handler at each site to show Henry while she watches from ringside.

They have a lot of fun on their travels together. Although most of Henry's travel is to dog shows, some is just for vacation. "We visit my parents, and I like to take Henry to New York to see the store windows at Christmas," says Cohen.

Henry won Best of Breed at Westminster in 2000. By his second Westminster, he had 57 group placements to his credit—an awesome record for a dog of a rare breed who hadn't been shown widely.

Suddenly, Henry was the favorite.

It's nerve-wracking for Cohen. She intently watches Henry in the ring. He looks great—confident and strong. His coat gleams in the lights.

Cohen has a whole group of friends sitting nearby and rooting for Henry.

Finally, the judge makes her decision. The Best of Breed Field Spaniel in 2001 is . . . Henry. Cohen and her friends scream with joy.

FANNY FACES HER OPPOSITION

Susan Hamil is worried. "Fanny came into Westminster as the number-one hound," says Hamil. "I was so nervous. When you're number one, there's no place to go but down."

It's hard for a top-winning show dog to perform well at the breed level. "It's the big bugaboo," says Hamil. "There's not as much excitement at the breed level, and these dogs thrive on excitement."

She's counting on handler Bruce Schultz to keep Fanny interested and happy. But Bruce was never supposed to be Fanny's handler.

Bruce's wife, Gretchen, was Fanny's constant companion from the day Fanny matured into a show girl. Gretchen had worked with Bloodhounds for many years, and has a special rapport with the breed. She's an athletic, curvaceous woman—and she and Fanny became an instantly recognizable pair.

Soon, Gretchen was handling Fanny through the "Battle of the Bitches." Ch. Sundown Alabaster Treasure JC (the Saluki) and Ch. Tryst of Grandeur (the Afghan) were in the hunt for number-one Hound. And a young Fanny was hot on their heels.

"Treasure and Tryst are so beautiful. They'd take shots of the two dogs in the sand with the wind blowing through their hair. They looked like art deco collectibles," says Hamil. Then she adds with her trademark humor, "And we looked like the Beverly Hillbillies." But Fanny held her own and placed in the Hound Group at Westminster in both 1999 and 2000.

Now Treasure and Tryst are semiretired and didn't come to Westminster. It might be Fanny's turn in the sun.

Fanny's career was a dream until December 1999. Then disaster struck. Gretchen Schultz injured her leg. Even after surgery, Gretchen couldn't handle a big dog like Fanny. Her husband Bruce took over the job.

Bruce is one of the nation's elite handlers—it's not like he didn't know how to show a Bloodhound. But Fanny, like most Bloodhounds, is an independent dog. She doesn't form close bonds quickly.

Bruce had to earn Fanny's trust. "Bruce had to work really hard at it," says Hamil. It didn't happen over night. It took a few months for them to become a real team. Eventually, it paid off. Bruce handled Fanny to 14 Best in Shows in 2000. "Now Fanny and Bruce have an even deeper bond than she and Gretchen had," says Hamil. "It's like Bruce is the only star in the sky."

Fanny follows that star into the Westminster Breed ring. They make a gorgeous team. Bruce is a handsome, brawny man with red-blond hair and beard. Fanny's head is up and her tail wags as she gazes at Bruce.

When the judging is over, Fanny wins Best of Breed. She'll be going on to the Hound Group that night. She's getting ready for a head-to-head battle with her major rival this year: Xena the Warrior Princess (Ch. Southchase's Warrior Princess). Fanny also has to worry about an Otterhound and 23 other Hounds who are hot on the trail of a possible Group win.

SOMETIMES A SHOW DOG IS MORE THAN JUST ANOTHER PRETTY FACE

After spending two days watching dogs being judged on their beauty, it's easy to think of them only in terms of their looks. But that would be a big mistake.

Many of these dogs are just a heartbeat—or a day—away from their working origins. Fanny the Bloodhound comes from a long line of dogs who perform search and rescue and law enforcement work. She has half-brothers and half-sisters who work for sheriff's departments.

Don't believe the rap that there isn't anything dumber on the end of a leash than a show dog. Some people claim that the Sporting breeds wouldn't know a rabbit in the field from a Volkswagen Rabbit in the garage, or that the herding dogs never come closer to a sheep than the wool sweaters they wear to keep cozy on Manhattan streets.

Last year there were a half million entries at AKC performance events. Even the primped, coifed canines at Westminster were part of the action. In fact, some of these dogs are so accomplished that they are the canine versions of a Miss America who teaches nuclear physics at Yale and makes the Olympic gymnastics team in her spare time.

Take Dual Champion Classic's Can Do Andrew. Andy really can do it all. This flashy orange and white Brittany is a Field Champion— beating out the best Brittanys that were bred purely for hunting. Andy's also one of the top Brittanys in the show ring, and he's handled by a 16-year-old.

Andy isn't the only dog with brains as well as beauty at the 2001 Westminster show. Forty-one entrants have hunting titles, 5 have earthdog titles, 54 have obedience titles, 21 have agility titles, 13 have herding titles, and a whopping 34 sight hounds have lure-coursing titles.

The Allure of Lure Coursing

Dual Champion Shema's Mia Sizzling Samba is a slender, leggy Pharaoh Hound. With its regal bearing and large, erect ears this ancient breed looks like the Egyptian god Anubis.

Sweet, compliant Samba becomes "a screaming maniac" when she chases the lure (a plastic bag has replaced the bunny) through a zigzag course. She's fast, agile, and driven. Samba has a Best in Field win—the performance equivalent of a Best in Show.

Peggy Sue Won Westminster; Her Mother Found the Rats

In 1995, Scottie breeder Camille Partridge wasn't dressed up in a fancy outfit while she watched the Best in Show competition. She was wearing her lucky earthdog T-shirt.

Ch. Gaelforce Post Script, the Scottish Terrier who was about to get the nod as Best in Show, was capturing the hearts of the crowd as she strutted around the ring on her short Scottie legs. She had the combination of dignity and joy that only a Terrier can muster. Peggy Sue came by her gameness honestly: Her mother, Ch. Glenlee's Sable Fox JE, was one of the very first dogs to ever earn an AKC earthdog title

If dog shows are a subculture, earthdog tests are akin to a cult. People involved in this sport excavate fields, place wooden tunnels inside holes, and then cover the entire area back up, making sure that it looks natural. They then spritz these tunnels with *rat tea*—a brew combining rat bedding mixed with water—so the dogs believe that a rat has left a trail to its lair. The dogs then make their way through elaborate mazes until they find their quarry—caged rats.

"Westminster was a big thrill, but nothing like earning that first earthdog title," says Partridge, who is now an AKC-approved earthdog judge. Breeders like Partridge ensure that the soul of these feisty little Terriers won't be lost in the glamour of the show ring.

Indy: She Didn't Stop at Best in Show

Indy the Doberman Pinscher survived bloat and won at Westminster in 1989. But that was pretty much just a warm-up.

Indy's official name became Ch. Royal Tudor's Wild As The Wind UDTX. Those four little letters at the end of Indy's name spell out a decade of accomplishment.

Competitive obedience is a lot more than the simple commands a dog learns in puppy kindergarten. To test the reliability of their training, advanced obedience dogs line up with a group of unfamiliar dogs and do a one-minute sit-stay and a five-minute-long down-stay while their owners leave the building. These complicated, mentally and physically challenging tasks—among others—garnered Indy the "UD" (for Utility Dog) after her name.

Fast forward to Indy at age 11, when she earned a Tracking Dog Excellent title. Indy had to follow the scent of a human over rough terrain, through cross-scents of other people, for up to 1,000 yards, and find three objects that a tracklayer had "lost." This title is one of the most difficult to earn in dogdom; fewer than 100 Tracking Dog Excellent titles are awarded in a typical year.

"When you pursue these activities, you have to take the time to know your dog inside," says Indy's owner, Susan Korp. "All of that beauty and all her titles—really and truly what made her special was what was inside of her."

Zap: A Bright Light

A Belgian Tervuren named Zap is one of the most titled dogs at the 2001 Westminster. Zap is officially known as Ch. Starbright Kilowatt CDX AX AXJ. The initials at the end of Zap's name attest to his string of agility and obedience titles.

Talk to owner Susan Young about Zap's accomplishments, and it doesn't take long for the conversation to turn personal. Young is a school teacher, and the handsome Herding dog with the rich mahogany coat frequently accompanies her to class. He reaches out to children who don't always respond to traditional teaching methods.

When Young's husband died, she turned to the big dog with the dark, keen eyes for solace. "Zap has become my protector. I know he grieves for George, just like I do," says Young.

In the middle of the glamour and hubbub of Westminster, Zap is a reminder that titles, trophies, and bragging rights aren't the most important thing. When you see Zap give Susan Young a look of gentle adoration, you know that this dog is more than just a pretty face.

EVERY DOG HAS HIS DAY

Westminster is a show within a show within a show. Some people come here hoping to grab the ultimate glory and make a place in dog show history. Others are pinching themselves just to be in Madison Square Garden. For some, showing dogs is a profession, while for others, it's an obsession. They're all here, in this famous arena, following their own dreams. They've become friends and competitors—some even fall in love with each other.

"These dogs represent so many different things to different people," says Dr. Kate An Hunter. "It's amazing the way dogs bring people together."

The clock is ticking away. It's nearly time to judge the Sporting, Hound, and Working Groups.

Front-runners like Fanny will hope for victory. The relative unknowns—like Henry the Field Spaniel and Tony the Otterhound—will hope for an upset.

Only one thing is certain: You never know what will happen at The Garden.

Chapter 11

The Magnificent Seven

The Garden is brightly lit again on Tuesday night. Huge floral arrangements, in Westminster's purple and gold colors, are placed in faux Grecian urns and artfully arranged across the stadium floor.

The press tables have a feeling of panic about them. Reporters have to get the story straight—and fast. The trouble is, only about half of them have ever been to a dog show before. On one side of the ring are tables for the print media. In past years, *Seattle Times* columnist Ranny Green was the unofficial dean of the Westminster press corps. He'd made sure that newcomers found the pressroom, and inconspicuously explained to sportswriters exactly what was going on during the show. Green's not here this year, so long-time pet writer Sue Jeffries from Oklahoma takes over in his place. She's sort of a media "mom," even introducing writers from local papers to exhibitors from their home states.

On the other side of the ring, photographers and television cameramen jostle for position. They are a lot more assertive than the print journalists. A few television reporters point out that they're "real" journalists, and have covered international hot spots such as the Balkans.

There is a lot of consternation over which journalists will sit at the prime press tables on the floor ringside, and which ones will be relegated to the nosebleed seats. A reporter is issued either a red button or a pale blue one to wear on her lapel. A blue button signifies major press, and gets you onto the floor where you can touch the dogs and interview the handlers. Those with red buttons aren't allowed on the floor.

The BBC, which was issued a red button, argues that it is major media and deserves a place at the table. On the other hand, *Dog News,* a weekly publication for the dog show set, and the Internet site *ThePoop.com* have no trouble getting seats at the table.

FIRST, THE NEXT GENERATION

Live, televised coverage of the show starts at 8:00. But on Tuesday night, pretty much everyone is in his seat by 7:00.

It's time to cheer on the junior showmanship finals. One hundred and twenty-one kids from across the country have competed over the past two days. Each junior handles his or her own dog. These dogs range from big, tough breeds like Akitas and Rottweilers to precious Papillons and rare Pulis. The youngest junior who qualifies for competition is 10 years old. The oldest— those competing for the last time—are 18.

By Tuesday night, the competition is narrowed down to eight finalists. These kids are good—really good. Every child handles his or her own dog flawlessly, showing the perfect gait and presenting each dog properly for his breed. As one by one, young handlers gait their dogs, the crowd whoops and cheers.

The winner is 16-year-old Elizabeth Jordan from San Jose, California, handling a Golden Retriever. "Elizabeth has been showing dogs since she was 3 years old," says jubilant mom Laurie Mashiko Jordan, herself a professional handler.

Elizabeth is poised as she calmly answers questions from the press. The pretty, slender young woman resembles a corporate CEO. Her silky black hair is pulled away from her face and she wears a business-like suit.

Elizabeth is handed her official, winning sash. She pulls it over her head. It reads: "The Westminster Kennel Club Best Junior Handler

2001." Elizabeth, smiling radiantly, sash across her chest, begins to look more like a beauty pageant winner than a CEO.

Most junior showmanship winners go on to become professional handlers. But whatever Elizabeth decides to do, the experience of showing a dog in front of 15,000 screaming fans—and a television audience of ten million people—will certainly stand her in good stead.

THE GOOD SPORTS

At precisely 8:00 p.m., the National Anthem plays over the loud speaker, and the Sporting dogs come into the ring.

The crowd roars its approval. The night of winning, losing, and making history has begun in earnest.

The Sporting breeds are the hunting dogs—fast-moving, leggy athletes and sweet spaniels alike.

Two dogs have been in a neck-and-neck race all year for top ranking in the group: a German Shorthaired Pointer called Megan (Ch. Khrispat's Megan A Point), and a German Wirehaired Pointer named Bentley (Ch. Wildfire's Bentley). Both are ranked in the top ten dogs of all breeds.

The big question on everyone's mind is which one of these two athletic dogs will win the group.

Of course, Judge Ralph Del Deo isn't "everyone." Tonight, only his opinion counts. Del Deo is an angular, white-haired attorney who has successfully argued a case before the U.S. Supreme Court. He isn't likely to be swayed by the crowd or the national rankings.

Del Deo works through the breeds methodically.

When he gets to Henry the Field Spaniel, he gives the dog an especially long look. Arlene Cohen's smile stretches across her face. That's her dog.

Welcome to Westminster

The volume turns up when Del Deo examines the Spinone Italiano. "Welcome to Westminster," he says. This is the first time this wire-haired, easygoing bird dog with hound-like ears has been eligible to compete. The crowd screams loudly when the dog gaits.

Producers at the USA Network probably aren't cheering along with the crowds at the appearance of the Spinone. In the past two years, the Jack Russell Terrier, Havanese, Lowchen, and Anatolian Shepherd—along with the Spinone—have been recognized by the AKC as eligible to compete in dog shows.

This is a big problem for people who bring you entertainment on the small screen. It takes about two minutes for a judge to evaluate a dog. Add five dogs to a show and suddenly you have another ten minutes of television time. The result is fewer minutes for features and less time to put the group judging in context. And there's not a thing that the USA Network can do about it.

Television producers' problems aren't on the minds of the crowd as they cheer for the adorable Spinone Italiano. Everyone likes to see a new dog in the ring.

◆ ◆

The Sporting Group

American Water Spaniel, Brittany, Chesapeake Bay Retriever, Clumber Spaniel, Cocker Spaniel, Curly-Coated Retriever, English Setter, English Cocker Spaniel, English Springer Spaniel, Field Spaniel, Flat-Coated Retriever, German Shorthaired Pointer, German Wirehaired Pointer, Golden Retriever, Gordon Setter, Irish Setter, Irish Water Spaniel, Labrador Retriever, Pointer, Spinone Italiano, Sussex Spaniel, Vizsla, Weimaraner, Welsh Springer Spaniel, and Wirehaired Pointing Griffon.

◆ ◆

THE FLASHY FLAT-COAT

One dog seems especially energized tonight. He's a Flat-Coated Retriever named Ch. Flatford Zeus the Major God JH.

When he gaits, Zeus springs into action, pulling on his leash as he flies across the ring. He's using every inch of space in the big arena, and the crowd loves it. He holds a perfect stack for the judge to admire and then leaps into the air with the sheer joy of being a dog.

The crowd gets behind Zeus and screams its approval as he moves across the ring. This dog just might put his nose somewhere between Megan's and Bentley's.

At the end of Zeus's name are the initials JH (Junior Hunter). He won't be judged on this, but Zeus has proven that he has the instinct and ability to retrieve game. This dog doesn't just *look* like a hunting dog, he *is* a hunting dog. Zeus can still perform what his breed was created to do.

Also, he's gorgeous.

There's another dog that's on fire: the Brittany. He moves out ahead of handler Clint Livingston, pulling on the end of his leash. This dog is ready for action.

The Cut

Del Deo isn't a demonstrative man. When it's time to make the cut, he walks along the lineup, growling out his decisions as he marches past the dogs. Del Deo walks past the Brittany. "Right here," he says. The Brittany's handler leaps up and takes the dog into the center of the ring. He's made the cut.

Del Deo continues down the line. "Right here," he says as he passes the Pointer. "Right here," he says to Megan, the German Shorthaired Pointer. "The Flat Coat," he says as he walks past Zeus. "The Golden," he says, already half a step past the dog. "The Clumber. The Springer." He looks at the Spinone Italiano, "Bring him out," he says. The crowd shouts its approval. Finally, Del Deo says, "The Weimaraner."

That's it. The cut's been made. The happy handlers have all brought their dogs out into the center of the ring so the judge can give them one final look.

Except the Golden.

The handler didn't hear the judge's call. No one in The Garden knows that Del Deo called out the Golden—they didn't hear him.

But millions of people in homes across America are screaming, "The Golden! The Golden!" The Group judging goes on without another look at the Golden Retriever.

It's noisy in The Garden, and handlers are paying a tremendous amount of attention to their dogs. At Westminster and other shows, every once in a while the handler doesn't hear the judge, and in the commotion of the moment the dog may be forgotten.

Live at Madison Square Garden, no one's thinking about the Golden. A lot of people are thinking about the German Wirehaired Pointer. One of the top dogs in the country just didn't make the cut.

That happens at The Garden.

Judge Ralph Del Deo has the dogs that remain in competition take one more run around the ring, one at a time. The feet of these athletic dogs fly across the floor. The crowd senses the drama—and the feeling that there might be an upset in the making.

Del Deo stands in front of the Flat-Coated Retriever and points. "One!" he says. He points to the German Shorthaired Pointer. "Two!" Then, the Brittany. "Three!" Finally, the Clumber Spaniel. "Four!"

Zeus the Major God has skipped over the pack and made his mark at Westminster. He did it because he showed the heart of a Sporting dog this night—athletic, exuberant, agile, eager, and fun.

There are those who speculate: Will Zeus the Major God meet the Coonhound Xena the Warrior Princess in the Best in Show ring? And if so, whose powers will be stronger?

GOOD SPORTSMANSHIP

Zeus's handler, Mark Bettis, receives congratulatory hugs from the other handlers in the ring. One friend is so exuberant that he almost knocks Bettis's glasses off his face.

Sportsmanship takes strange twists among dog handlers. You want your dog to win. A popular book even gives little techniques on how to "psyche out" your opposition. Tricks include looking at your opponent's dog and then shaking your head sadly, or acting as if you're going to elbow your way into the ring first, then stepping back suddenly so your competitor finds herself unexpectedly at the front of the line.

Certainly, there's gamesmanship in dog shows, just like any other sport. But more often than not, there's genuine support for one another. If you're a professional handler, most of your friends are professional handlers as well.

And friends help one another out.

Consider the Best in Show competition at Westminster in 1993. Your cynicism will melt.

Friendly Competitors

The number-one dog going into Westminster that year was a Springer Spaniel named Ch. Salilyn's Condor (called Robert). Mark Threlfall was his handler.

"I'd been in about 150 Best in Show rings with Robert. You'd think I would be used to this by now, but I was conscious of my heart beating fast. Best in Show at Westminster is different," admits Threlfall, a square, muscular man who now works in dog-related public relations and broadcasting.

Robert was the odds-on favorite going into the show, but at Westminster anything can happen.

For Robert, that "anything" looked like it might be a young German Shepherd Dog called Mystique (Ch. Altana's Mystique). Threlfall's best friend, Jimmy Moses, handled Mystique. "Jimmy was a big fan of Robert, and I was a big fan of Mystique," says Threlfall. "Before we went into the Best in Show ring, I said to him, 'Well, Jimmy, if it's not me, I hope it's you.'"

The young German Shepherd bitch was just coming into her own, and Moses replied, "I want to win next year."

It's hot on the floor of Westminster. Sizzling hot. The handlers of athletic breeds—breeds such as shepherds and Springers—run flat out around the big ring and work up a sweat. Both Threlfall and Moses—two of the best in the business—were showing their dogs to perfection. "I looked over to Jimmy and said to him, 'For a guy who doesn't want to win, you're sure working awfully hard,'" says Threlfall.

Both handlers were sweating. Their dogs were getting warm. Threlfall gave Robert some water from a bottle he'd brought into the ring. Then he looked over at Jimmy Moses and Mystique. The dog was panting, and Moses hadn't brought in any water.

Mark Threlfall could have smiled to himself, smug in the knowledge that his dog had an edge. But he didn't.

"I went over and gave my water bottle to Jimmy for Mystique," he says.

In 1993, a good guy finished first. Judge Barbara Heller pointed to Threlfall and Robert. "I swear this is true. She's a soft-spoken woman and I wasn't sure what she said. I jumped up, but I was thinking that if she said 'German Shepherd' I'm the biggest fool in the world."

Threlfall wasn't mistaken—Robert had just received the nod for Best in Show.

Why would Mark Threlfall jeopardize winning Westminster by giving his competitor's dog water? "Jimmy and I are friends," he answers. "We're going to be friends long after Robert and Mystique are gone."

Mystique went on to become the top-winning show dog of all time, although she never won Westminster. The show records of Robert and Mystique will go down in the history of the sport.

What went on between two friends in the Best in Show ring that day won't receive a trophy or an engraved plaque. That simple act of sportsmanship wasn't reported in the press. It didn't make headlines. It was just a small moment in America's most dramatic dog show.

Sometimes, it's not just the dogs who show grace under pressure.

THE HOUNDS OF WESTMINSTER

While cameras flash on the Sporting Group winner and Mark Bettis answers questions from the "pup"arazzi, the Hounds are called into the ring.

Hounds are dogs who hunt by scent or sight, and include breeds as disparate as the long and low Dachshund and the enormous Irish Wolfhound.

♦ ♦ ♦ ♦ ♦ ♦ ♦ ♦ ♦ ♦ ♦ ♦ ♦ ♦ ♦ ♦ ♦ ♦ ♦ ♦

The Hound Group

Afghan Hound, Basenji, Basset Hound, Beagle (not exceeding 13 inches), Beagle (over 13 inches but not exceeding 15 inches), Black and Tan Coonhound, Bloodhound, Borzoi, Longhaired Dachshund, Smooth Dachshund, Wirehaired Dachshund, American Foxhound, English Foxhound, Greyhound, Harrier, Ibizan Hound, Irish Wolfhound, Norwegian Elkhound, Otterhound, Petite Basset Griffon Vendeen, Pharaoh Hound, Rhodesian Ridgeback, Saluki, Scottish Deerhound, and Whippet.

♦ ♦ ♦ ♦ ♦ ♦ ♦ ♦ ♦ ♦ ♦ ♦ ♦ ♦ ♦ ♦ ♦ ♦ ♦ ♦

Judge Kent Delaney looks festive. He's wearing a well-cut tuxedo with a blue brocade vest. While many judges are quite solemn, and some are downright dour, Delaney is all smiles and exuberance. He's one of the most popular judges in the country, both for his friendly demeanor and his encyclopedic knowledge of dogs. Make no mistake about it: Delaney has a happy grin on his face and a gentle hand with the dogs, but he also has a very sharp eye for canine faults and virtues.

Fanny's Fans

"You think baseball players are superstitious?" asks Fanny's owner, Susan Hamil. "You have no idea." Everyone in Fanny's camp is wearing pink and black. They're Fanny's colors. "Gretchen Schultz has rules about colors," explains Hamil. "No red, no white, no yellow." Tonight, you'd better be wearing pink and black for Fanny.

Hamil wears a pink sweater decorated with black dogs. Her husband John wears a pink and black tie. Gretchen herself isn't taking any chances: She's wearing two pink and black sweaters, one layered over the other.

Kent Delaney has liked Fanny in past shows—he has given her a Group First and a Best in Show in previous years. But this makes Hamil worry.

"If Fanny doesn't show well, he's going to think of the times when he's seen her and she looked so much better."

Fanny isn't the only dog in the group whom Delaney's given top honors to. And maybe this time, he'll be intrigued by a fresh face he hasn't seen before. The worries are endless. Thank goodness everyone remembered to wear the right colors.

The Otterhound Fan Club

The clothing crisis for Tony the Otterhound's owner has been resolved. Joellen is wearing a handsome suit that looks very professional. "We all got dressed up to watch Tony in the Group," says Dr. Kate An Hunter. "We even had champagne served at our seats. I thought the champagne was pretty good, but it might have just been the atmosphere."

A couple of times during the group judging, a camera zooms in on Tony and shows his sweet, shaggy face and displays him on the overhead monitor. This brings big cheers from the Otterhound faithful.

"We knew the Bloodhound was favored, but we hoped against hope that Tony would win something," says Hunter.

AN ENTERTAINING GROUP

Kent Delaney's enthusiasm for the dogs spreads to the crowds. When he examines the Basset Hound, he gets down on his hands and knees and gives the dog his full attention. When he watches a dog gait, it's as though there's nothing else in the universe.

The crowd screams for its favorites. If they had an applause-o-meter, Fanny would be at the top of it. But there are a lot of great dogs.

There are some dogs who are stars outside the show ring, but that won't affect Delaney's judging. The Scottish Deerhound and the Pharaoh Hound are both Dual Champions in lure coursing and conformation. Tony the Otterhound has agility titles, attesting to his athleticism. The Petite Basset Griffon Vendeen (usually called a PBGV) is co-owned by baseball great Ken Caminiti, who also co-owns the Brittany who won a Group Third in the Sporting Group.

The cut

Delaney makes his cut: the Afghan Hound, the 15-inch Beagle, the Basset Hound, the Bloodhound, the Wirehaired Dachshund, the Irish Wolfhound, the Norwegian Elkhound, the Petite Basset Griffon Vendeen, the Scottish Deerhound, and the Whippet.

The big surprise is that the Coonhound, Xena the Warrior Princess, didn't make the cut.

Fanny puts on the best performance of her life. She's animated and wagging her tail. But the other dogs are having great shows, too. The Afghan springs across the floor with an elastic gait of incredible grace. The little PBGV has a lovable, disheveled face and a sound, rugged little body. Every one of the dogs who made the cut is looking great.

Kent Delaney has each one gait alone, one last time. He points to Fanny, telling Bruce Schultz to move by the number one sign—then Delaney breaks into a huge grin and shakes Bruce's hand. Fanny has won the Hound Group.

Next, Delaney picks out the Afghan Hound and shakes her handler's hand. He does the same for the PBGV and the Irish Wolfhound.

The crowd responds enormously. The surprise handshake, Kent Delaney's obvious joy about judging the dogs he loves, the popular winner—all this has brought the sense of celebration up a notch.

Susan Hamil is overjoyed. She remembers the day that she picked out Fanny as a puppy. She remembers knowing this dog had stardust, that she was different from the rest. And now she's won the Hound Group at Westminster. "I can't imagine what it would be like winning

Best in Show," says Hamil. "It would be completely impossible for me to be more elated."

Fanny won't have a lot of time to rest on her laurels. There's just one more group to go before Best in Show.

LIFE IMITATING ART IMITATING LIFE

It begins to sink in: The real-life Westminster Kennel Club show is beginning to look an awful lot like its spoof. Since the movie *Best in Show* came out a few months previously, it's all anyone can talk about. The movie is a "mockumentary" (or, alternatively, a "dogumentary") that pokes fun at the foibles of the fictional Mayflower Kennel Club Dog Show.

The movie follows four dogs into the Best in Show ring: a Bloodhound, a Shih Tzu, a white Standard Poodle, and a Norwich Terrier. Now, two of those breeds are in the real Westminster Best in Show lineup, while a white Standard Poodle came in second in the Non-Sporting Group. Out of 158 breeds and varieties, the coincidences are astounding.

TV Guide further blurred the lines between real life and the movies when their pre-Westminster edition included a feature that had real life host David Frei and movie "host" Fred Willard commenting on the virtues of various dogs.

A lot of dog show people who saw the movie were horrified by it. "It makes it seem that everyone who attends dog shows is neurotic, has two left feet, is gay, or is sleeping around," says one viewer who gave it a "paws down" rating. Others found it hilarious, pointing out that the humor was at the expense of the people, not the dogs.

It's the only Hollywood movie that has ever got the details right about a dog show. The actors went to dog-show handling classes, and a lot of the minor parts were played by real dog show people.

And the Bloodhound who was one of the stars of the movie? He's Fanny's half-brother.

KEEP THOSE DOGGIES MOVING!

There's just one more step before Best in Show: the Herding Group. These dogs herd anything that will move in a flock—sheep, cattle, ducks, goats, even the occasional small child.

◆ ◆

The Herding Group

Australian Cattle Dog, Australian Shepherd, Bearded Collie, Belgian Malinois, Belgian Sheepdog, Belgian Tervuren, Border Collie, Bouvier des Flandres, Briard, Canaan Dog, Rough Collie, Smooth Collie, German Shepherd Dog, Old English Sheepdog, Puli, Shetland Sheepdog, Welsh Corgi Cardigan, and Welsh Corgi Pembroke.

◆ ◆

There's a prohibitive favorite in this group: Bebe (Ch. Coventry Queue), a foxy-faced Pembroke Welsh Corgi. Bebe won the Group at Westminster last year, and she's the number-three dog in the country, hot on the heels of dog number two, Joey the Shih Tzu.

Still, some top dogs have gone by the wayside tonight, not even making the cut. There's certainly no guarantee that Bebe is going to earn the blue ribbon. It's not that easy at Westminster.

Panting

Judge Kathleen Steen has raised some serious eyebrows. She's decked out in a gorgeous outfit, and her hair and nails are meticulously done. The cuffs and neckline of her jacket are outlined with sparkling silver. By any standard, she looks incredibly elegant. There's just one issue: Steen's beautiful outfit isn't a dress or a skirt ensemble—instead, it's palazzo pants. No one can remember a female judge who wore pants. Maybe tradition at Westminster is easing just a bit.

Big Heart, Short Legs

When the dogs start moving, Bebe looks fabulous. She exudes confidence. She moves really fast on her short Corgi legs; her handler, Michael Scott, runs behind the smiling little dog. Bebe is co-owned by Mrs. Alan Robson, one of the great dog names of all time. A Pointer she owned went Best in Show at Westminster in 1985; five other dogs—another Pointer, a Wirehaired Dachshund, a Dalmatian, a Poodle, and Bebe—have been in the Best in Show lineup a total of eight times.

But Bebe's not the only dog showing the style of a great herding dog. The Australian Shepherd is athletic and lithe— you can imagine him moving a herd of stubborn sheep or cattle. The Aussie is owner-handled, and there hasn't been an owner-handled dog picked to win a group all night. This might be the one.

The Smooth Collie is exceptionally athletic-looking. Maybe it's time for a Collie to win again at The Garden—and this time to have a happy ending.

The German Shepherd Dog is the sentimental favorite. This dog was found tied up and neglected, the story goes. Now she's one of the top show dogs in the country, receiving lots of exercise, love, and pampering.

The Cut

Steen makes her cut. She pulls out the Australian Shepherd, the Bearded Collie, the Briard (a flashy French herding breed with long, flowing hair), the Smooth Collie, the German Shepherd Dog, the Puli, the Shetland Sheepdog, and Bebe, the Pembroke Welsh Corgi.

Mark Bettis, who handled the Flat Coated Retriever to the Sporting Group win earlier in the evening, is handling the Bearded Collie. If the Beardie wins the Herding Group, he'll have to decide which dog to handle, and which one will be handled by an assistant or by another handler. Handling a lot of top flight dogs— which many handlers do—can be a serious juggling act.

Steen has the dogs move around one last time.

Then she points her elegant hand at Bebe. "One!" she says. Then the Shetland Sheepdog, "Two!" The Australian Shepherd, "Three!" and the Smooth Collie, "Four!"

Bebe has a shot at Best in Show.

THE MAGNIFICENT SEVEN

Now they are seven. And what a magnificent seven: Rocky, the workmanlike Standard Schnauzer; Mick, the British Kerry Blue Terrier with the unmistakable aura; Joey, the Shih Tzu who's a rhinestone cowboy; J.R., the Bichon with the exclamation point at the end of his name; Zeus, the Flat-Coated Retriever who's become a Major God in the world of dogs; Fanny, the Bloodhound with star quality; and Bebe, the foxy-faced Corgi who thinks she owns the world.

People who have been coming to Westminster for 50 years say this is the finest lineup for Best in Show they've ever seen. These are seven dogs in their prime. These dogs have withstood the test of competition. They aren't going to be intimidated by the crowd. And they are showing better than ever before.

It's a moving experience to see these dogs up close and personal, just as it's better to see a great performer live than on television. These seven dogs have a presence, a life force, and a sparkle that you can't get out of your mind.

Four years ago, Susan Hamil went to a remote Texas ranch and picked out Fanny, the unforgettable puppy with stardust. Six other breeders and owners saw the same kind of intangible, special quality in their dogs.

But only one of these great dogs will be named the top dog at the most prestigious dog show on earth.

It's time for Best in Show.

Chapter 12

Top Dog

Best in Show judge Dorothy Macdonald has been sequestered for the past two days. She has no idea which dogs have been winning, and which ones have fallen along the way.

When she finally walks out onto the floor, Macdonald likes what she sees. "There were seven quality dogs out there," she says. She agrees it's one of the best lineups that has ever been assembled. Macdonald has a distinct, bell-like voice that reflects her British roots. "Any one of those dogs could justifiably win," she says.

Macdonald says that, in some ways, the quality of the dogs made her job easier. "I couldn't really go wrong. I was lucky—the only thing I really had to worry about was falling down and tripping on my dress."

Although Macdonald is a friendly, approachable woman with a self-deprecating sense of humor, when it comes to judging dogs she's passionate. Macdonald is a serious student of dog breeds. Talk with her for more than a few minutes, and you'll end up learning things you never knew: what the Greek writers had to say about dogs, what influence Marco Polo had on the development of breeds, the fact that Kubla Kahn had 5,000 fighting dogs in a division of his army.

Dorothy Macdonald isn't going to make a whimsical decision. And she isn't going to trip over her dress.

While she's taking a good look at the dogs in front of her, the crowd is getting louder and louder.

"The floor down there shakes," reports Susan Hamil. "A lot of dogs would fold their tent and say, 'I'm out of here.' It's like an Olympic athlete who chokes." Just like the great Olympians do better in the competitive climate of the games, a great show dog gets better as the show progresses.

This year, seven dogs were each giving the performance of a lifetime.

Zeus moves like the Sporting dog he is, full of energy and vitality. Fanny wags her tail at Bruce, moving in strong, sure strides. When she finishes gaiting, Bruce reaches down and kisses her on the nose.

Rocky, the Standard Schnauzer, is sure-footed and serious. Mick moves like a little stallion, revved up by the crowd. J.R., his bright, black eyes shiny with excitement, leads Scott Sommer around the ring. Bebe is foxy-faced and sassy—you can just imagine this little dog telling some full-sized cows where they'd better go. And Joey skims over the ground, his silky fur shimmering in the light.

THE ESSENCE OF THE BREED

Macdonald looks at each dog differently. Each dog should be built, should move, and should relate to people based on the job he was bred to do, and the place he had to do it in.

She dismisses people who talk about the traits of a show dog. "There is no such thing as a generic show dog," she says emphatically. You can only judge a dog in the context of what he was bred to do. Even if he was just bred to be a companion, you can judge how well his body and personality allow him to do that job.

"Every breed has an essence," says Macdonald. "The soul of that breed should look out at you in that dog's face."

Macdonald takes a final look at the lineup, giving each one a long gaze. She's made up her mind.

She walks deliberately over to the judge's table, writes down a dog breed and an armband number, and picks up the Best in Show ribbon. At other dog shows, the Best in Show ribbon is red, white, and blue. At Westminster, the enormous rosette is the club's colors: purple and gold.

Westminster Kennel Club President Chet Collier and Show Chairman Ron Menaker carry the big trophies.

Macdonald stands in front of the seven dogs. She says two words: "The Bichon."

The "Pup"arazzi

Pandemonium breaks out. J.R. senses the news is good, and starts barking excitedly. He waves his front paws enthusiastically at the hub-bub around him.

Then the wave of the press runs into the ring. Princess Diana didn't face paparazzi any more daunting than the Westminster "pup"arazzi. Dozens of reporters call out questions as countless cameras flash.

"It was quite an ordeal," says Sommer. "They wanted me to turn J.R. around in the bowl, facing a particular direction. But my assistant, Dennis, was trapped in the crowd—there wasn't anyone for J.R. to focus on. It was overwhelming."

Sommer looks a little bit panicked, but not J.R. He waves at the hoards of reporters, having a good time. Finally Sommer grabs J.R. and runs out of the ring.

Channel 10 reporter Jennifer Madden hasn't joined the madding crowd that surrounds Sommer. Instead, she's positioned herself right by the ring exit. When Sommer tries to get out of the ring, she snares him for a brief, but exclusive, interview. "I figured it was no different than covering a fire," she says. "He was going to have to come out sometime, and I was at the only exit."

THE DECISION

"All the dogs were beautiful," says Macdonald. "There wasn't any process of narrowing down my decision. There just wasn't a second-place dog." She says that she came to the conclusion that, of all the dogs that day, J.R. best epitomized breed type. "He was the essence of what a Bichon should be," she says. "He was as near to perfection as you can get."

Through all the excitement—the crowds, the noise, the lights—J.R. is having a fabulous time. He soaks up all the attention. He waves to all his new friends. His bright, dark eyes shine with the joy of the moment. As long as Scott Sommer is with him, J.R. is happy and ready for action—the soul and essence of a companion dog.

This year, Ch. Special Times Just Right!—the dog with the exclamation point—earned dogdom's Holy Grail. He beat the best of the best, from America and around the globe.

J.R. rose to the challenges of the noise, the crowds, the heat, and the tension that fills The Garden. He skipped through the competition full of verve and charm.

This Bichon is already becoming a household name—J.R., the little white dog who waves. Ch. Special Times Just Right!—J.R.—is America's top dog.

At least until next year.

Epilogue

Six Months Later

Ch. Special Times Just Right! (J.R.) lives fulltime with his handler, Scott Sommer, and attends shows with Sommer and his crew. "The only thing that's different [now] is that he isn't going into the ring," says Sommer. J.R. remains in perfect show trim.

The Bichon is recognized everywhere. "Each time he waves his paws, someone says, "That's J.R.!" and they want to meet him," says Sommer.

Ch. Torum's Scarf Michael (Mick) is the number one dog in the country. He has accumulated well over twice as many points as his nearest rival. Mick started his post-Westminster career on February 19, 2001—just six days after the big event. At that show, Mick received the winning nod for Best in Show. The judge? None other than Dorothy Macdonald.

Bernice Kusch, who owned Mick's ancestor Callaghan (the dog who won Crufts and was never returned to America), got a new puppy this year. He's Mick's son. Just as Callaghan revitalized and improved Kerry Blue Terriers in England two decades ago, Mick is doing the same for the breed today in America. For Kusch, things have come full circle.

Ch. Charisma Jailhouse Rock (Rocky) is in a pack of dogs vying for the number two ranking in America, after Mick.

Ch. Charing Cross Ragtime Cowboy (Joey) retired from show biz after Westminster. His fur has been clipped into a comfy, short hairdo. Joey has adjusted happily to life with kennel manager and co-breeder Barbara Finanger. At night, Joey sleeps in the same bed as Barbara, her husband, and two other Shih Tzu. Joey's legacy is already appearing in the ring. His son, Ch. Hallmark Jolei Raggedy Andy, has earned 15 Best in Shows since Westminster and is one of the top ten dogs in the country.

Ch. Ridgerunner Unforgettable (Fanny) was weaned gradually from her show life. "We took six weeks to help her make the transition," says owner Susan Hamil. At first, Fanny went to a couple of shows just to hang out. When Fanny got used to life off the road, she came home to live with Susan and John Hamil. If Fanny passes all her genetic tests with flying colors, Susan may consider breeding her.

Kent Delaney had a serious heart attack after judging at the Whippet National Specialty show in April 2001. After a lengthy convalescence, Delaney began judging again at the end of September 2001.

Ch. Sundown Alabaster Treasure JC (Treasure), the Saluki, had a litter of three puppies. Karen Black now takes 9-month-old Sundown Party at St. Tropez (called Tropez) to handling class. She hopes that he'll be her next partner in the show ring. Treasure still shows occasionally at specialty (all-Saluki) shows. She recently won Best of Opposite Sex from the Veteran's class.

Ch. Eli-Fran's Sir William (Willie), the English Toy Spaniel who won an Award of Merit at Westminster, won Best in Show at the English Toy Spaniel Club of America national specialty in May 2001.

Ch. Cheri-a Lady Isabella Smokey Valley (Shower) didn't attend the English Toy Spaniel national specialty this year. Owners Jerry Elliott and John Wood planned to retire her. But when the Westminster judges for 2002 were announced in May, Jerry and John recognized a slate of judges that have liked Shower in the past. They are considering one more attempt at Westminster.

Ch. Marshfield's Boys' Night Out (Henry) is currently the top-winning Field Spaniel of all time. He's earned seven Best in Shows since Westminster, and has won the Field Spaniel national specialty show for the second year. Henry is still a full-time family pet, and never goes to a dog show without Arlene.

Ch. Whipperinn's Virgil J., the English Foxhound who was upset at Westminster, won Best in Show at the first national specialty show of the English Foxhound Club of America. Dr. William Newman, Virgil's backer, is considering sponsoring a couple of promising young dogs that he thinks will represent the next generation of the sport.

Westminster Kennel Club Dog Show Best in Show Winners

1877–1906: There was no Best in Show award, which was typical of the dog shows of the time.

1907: Ch. Warren Remedy, Smooth Fox Terrier

1908: Ch. Warren Remedy, Smooth Fox Terrier

1909: Ch. Warren Remedy, Smooth Fox Terrier

1910: Ch. Sabine Rarebit, Smooth Fox Terrier

1911: Ch. Tickle-Em-Jock, Scottish Terrier

1912: Ch. Kenmare Sorceress, Airedale Terrier

1913: Ch. Strathtay Prince Albert, Bulldog

1914: Ch. Slumber, Old English Sheepdog

1915: Ch. Matford Vic, Wire Fox Terrier

1916: Ch. Matford Vic, Wire Fox Terrier

1917: Ch. Conejo Wycollar Boy, Wire Fox Terrier

1918: Ch. Haymarket Fautless, Bull Terrier

1919: Ch. Briergate Bright Beauty, Airedale Terrier

1920: Ch. Conejo Wycollar Boy, Wire Fox Terrier

1921: Ch. Midkiff Seductive, Cocker Spaniel

1922: Ch. Boxwood Barkentine, Airedale Terrier

1923: No Best in Show: The American Kennel Club barred awarding Best in Show awards during 1923, while it developed comprehensive new rules for Group and Best in Show judging.

1924: Ch. Barberryhill Bootlegger, Sealyham Terrier

1925: Ch. Governor Moscow, Pointer

1926: Ch. Signal Circuit of Halleston, Wire Fox Terrier

1927: Ch. Pinegrade Perfection, Sealyham Terrier

1928: Ch. Talavera Margaret, Wire Fox Terrier

1929: Laund Loyalty of Bellhaven, Collie

1930: Ch. Pendley Calling of Blarney, Wire Fox Terrier

1931: Ch. Pendley Calling of Blarney, Wire Fox Terrier

1932: Ch. Nancolleth Markable, Pointer

1933: Warland Protector of Shelterock, Airedale Terrier

1934: Ch. Flornell Spicy Bit of Halleston, Wire Fox Terrier

1935: Ch. Nunsoe Duc de la Terrace of Blakeen, Standard Poodle

1936: Ch. St. Margaret Magnificent of Clairedale, Sealyham Terrier

1937: Ch. Flornell Spicypiece of Halleston, Wire Fox Terrier

1938: Daro of Marido, English Setter

1939: Ch. Ferry von Rauhfelsen of Giralda, Doberman Pinscher

1940: Ch. My Own Brucie, Cocker Spaniel

1941: Ch. My Own Brucie, Cocker Spaniel

1942: Ch. Wolvey Pattern of Edgerstoune, West Highland White Terrier

1943: Ch. Pitter Patter of Piperscroft, Miniature Poodle

1944: Ch. Flornell Rare-Bit of Twin Ponds, Welsh Terrier

1945: Shieling's Signature, Scottish Terrier

1946: Ch. Hetherington Model Rhythm, Wire Fox Terrier

1947: Ch. Warlord of Mazelaine, Boxer

1948: Ch. Rock Ridge Night Rocket, Bedlington Terrier

1949: Ch. Mazelaine's Zazarac Brandy, Boxer

1950: Ch. Walsing Winning Trick of Edgerstoune, Scottish Terrier

1951: Ch. Bang Away of Sirrah Crest, Boxer

1952: Ch. Rancho Dobe's Storm, Doberman Pinscher

1953: Ch. Rancho Dobe's Storm, Doberman Pinscher

1954: Ch. Carmor's Rise and Shine, Cocker Spaniel

1955: Ch. Kippax Fearnought, Bulldog

1956: Ch. Wilber White Swan, Toy Poodle

1957: Ch. Shirkhan of Grandeur, Afghan Hound

1958: Ch. Puttencove Promise, Standard Poodle

1959: Ch. Frontclair Festoon, Miniature Poodle

1960: Ch. Chik T'Sun of Caversham, Pekingese

1961: Ch. Cappoquin Little Sister, Toy Poodle

1962: Ch. Elfinbrook Simon, West Highland White Terrier

1963: Ch. Wakefield's Black Knight, English Springer Spaniel

1964: Ch. Courtenay Fleetfoot of Pennyworth, Whippet

1965: Ch. Carmichaels Fanfare, Scottish Terrier

1966: Ch. Zeloy Mooremaides Magic, Wire Fox Terrier

1967: Ch. Bardene Bingo, Scottish Terrier

1968: Ch. Stingray of Derryabah, Lakeland Terrier

1969: Ch. Glamoor Good News, Skye Terrier

1970: Ch. Arriba's Prima Donna, Boxer

1971: Ch. Chinoe's Adamant James, English Springer Spaniel

1972: Ch. Chinoe's Adamant James, English Springer Spaniel

1973: Ch. Acadia Command Performance, Standard Poodle

1974: Ch. Gretchenhof Columbia River, German Shorthaired Pointer

1975: Ch. Sir Lancelot of Barvan, Old English Sheepdog

1976: Ch. Jo Ni's Red Baron of Crofton, Lakeland Terrier

1977: Ch. Dersade Bobby's Girl, Sealyham Terrier

1978: Ch. Cede Higgins, Yorkshire Terrier

1979: Ch. Oak Tree's Irishtocrat, Irish Water Spaniel

1980: Ch. Innisfree's Sierra Cinnar, Siberian Husky

1981: Ch. Dhandy's Favorite Woodchuck, Pug

1982: Ch. St. Aubrey Dragonora of Elsdon, Pekingese

1983: Ch. Kabiks the Challenger, Afghan Hound

1984: Ch. Seaward's Blackbeard, Newfoundland

1985: Ch. Braeburn's Close Encounter, Scottish Terrier

1986: Ch. Marjetta's National Acclaim, Pointer

1987: Ch. Covy Tucker Hill's Manhattan, German Shepherd Dog

1988: Ch. Great Elms Prince Charming, Pomeranian

1989: Ch. Royal Tudor's Wild as the Wind CD, Doberman Pinscher

1990: Ch. Wendessa Crown Prince, Pekingese

1991: Ch. Whisperwind on a Carousel, Standard Poodle

1992: Ch. Registry's Lonesome Dove, Wire Fox Terrier

1993: Ch. Salilyn's Condor, English Springer Spaniel

1994: Ch. Chidley Willum the Conqueror, Norwich Terrier

1995: Ch. Gaelforce Post Script, Scottish Terrier

1996: Ch. Clussexx Country Sunrise, Clumber Spaniel

1997: Ch. Parsifal Di Casa Netzer, Standard Schnauzer

1998: Ch. Fairewood Frolic, Norwich Terrier

1999: Ch. Loteki Supernatural Being, Papillon

2000: Ch. Salilyn 'N Erin's Shameless, English Springer Spaniel

2001: Ch. Special Times Just Right!, Bichon Frise

Source: Westminster Kennel Club publications

Appendix II

Resources

....

If you're interested in learning more about the Westminster Kennel Club, dog shows, or purebred dogs, here are some sources of information to get you started:

THE WESTMINSTER KENNEL CLUB

Web site: The Westminster Kennel Club has an outstanding Web site (**www.westminsterkennelclub.org**). The site includes a lot of information about the show's history and provides great links to other dog sites. The official show catalog is posted on the first day of competition each year, and the club gives regular updates on winners in the breed, group, and Best in Show. The marked calendars from previous years allow you to click and see pictures of breed winners, group placers, and Best in Show.

Book: In 2001, the Westminster Kennel Club self-published *The Dog Show: 125 Years of Westminster* by club member and former AKC president William F. Stifle (240 pages, $50 plus $10 shipping and handling). This serious tome gives an exhaustive history of the Westminster Kennel Club. It includes lists of all club members from the time of its formation in 1877, as well as annual accountings of the shows, and pictures of Best in Show winners. There are over 350 photographs in this coffee-table book. To order, go to the Westminster Kennel Club Web site at **www.westminsterkennelclub.org.**

THE USA NETWORK

The USA Network covers the group judging and Best in Show live every year, telecasting from 8:00 to 11:00 p.m. on the show dates. The coverage is lively, informed, and compelling—and it gives great close-ups of dogs and people. USA Network reports that an estimated 10 million viewers watch the telecast every year.

THE AMERICAN KENNEL CLUB

The AKC registers over one million purebred dogs each year and is the licensing organization for dog shows.

Web site: For more information about purebred dogs, dog shows, and breed standards, go to the American Kennel Club's informative Web site, **www.akc.org.** When you click on information about specific breeds, the page includes the official breed standard and links to the breed club and breed rescue. You can also order brochures that explain how dog shows work, supply rules and regulations for various events, and provide other useful information.

The Complete Dog Book, 19th Edition revised. This weighty book is the AKC "bible." It includes a history and breed standard for every recognized breed (Hungry Minds, Inc., 790 pages, $32.95).

AKC Gazette. The *Gazette* is the official magazine of the AKC. This excellent publication includes columns that relate to specific breeds in every issue, news from the world of shows, and articles about breeding, handling, and training, among other topics. A subscription includes a copy of the *AKC Events Calendar,* which lists all upcoming dog shows, obedience trials, agility trials, field events, earthdog tests, and other AKC activities. Annual subscription: $29.93.

American Kennel Club Awards. This magazine provides a comprehensive record of placements, awards, and titles in conformation and other AKC events. This is a magazine for people who are seriously keeping track of who's doing what in the dog-show world. Annual subscription: $69.

JUST FOR FUN

Best in Show is the hilarious "mockumentary" about winning the fictional Mayflower Kennel Club Dog Show. It's available at video stores nationwide.

Dog Eat Dog: A Very Human Book About Dogs and Dog Shows by Jane and Michael Stern is entertaining nonfiction that follows a Bullmastiff breeder through a year of showing dogs, culminating with a chapter on Westminster.

SHOW MAGAZINES

There are a wide variety of magazines devoted to dogs, dog breeds, and dog activities. The pages of these publications are full of ads for the nation's top show dogs.

The Canine Chronicle. **www.caninechronicle.com.** 3622 NE Jacksonville Road, Ocala, FL 34479, 352-369-1104. Annual subscription: $80.

Dogs in Review. **www.dogsinreview.com.** P.O. Box 30430, Santa Barbara, CA 93130, 805-692-2045. Annual subscription: $48.

Dog News. **www.dognews.com.** 1115 Broadway, New York, NY 10010, 212-462-9588. Annual subscription: $150 (50 issues).

ShowSight Magazine. **www.dmcg.com/pubs/showsight.** Doll-McGinnis Publications, 8848 Beverly Hills, Lakeland, FL 33809, 863-858-3939. Annual subscription: $60.

DOG SHOW HISTORY

Dog Shows: 1930–1949 by Bert Morgan is a sumptuous photographic record that captures the nostalgic charm and glamour of the dog shows of that era.

Dog Shows Then and Now by Anne Hier. The serious fancier will be interested in this comprehensive overview of the sport, including selected British and American articles from the past 159 years, extensive annotations, and a bibliography.

HOW-TO BOOKS AND VIDEOS

This is a partial listing of some of the books and videos that give advice on the world of dog shows. The most comprehensive dog book and video source is Dogwise, a small company that prides itself on its selection of books and knowledgable staff. You'll find them on the Web at **www.dogwise com,** or you can order their catalog by calling 800-776-2665.

Books

Born to Win: Breed to Succeed by Patricia Craige presents a plan for the committed breeder for breeding, conditioning, showing, and working with mentors and newcomers.

Dog Showing for Beginners by Lynn Hall is designed for a newcomer to the show world, with information on finding the right breed, breeder, dog, clubs, and matches, as well as understanding the point system, what equipment to buy, playing politics, looking like a pro, and having fun.

Kennelwood's Beginning Conformation Training is a good beginner's guide to understanding dog shows, with information about how to train you and your puppy to do it right.

Show Me! A Dog-Showing Primer by D. Caroline Coile gives advice on how to choose, raise, and train a show dog and how to train yourself to be a good handler.

Tricks of the Trade: From Best Intentions to Best in Show by Pat Hastings gives practical ideas for showing your dog, from the whelping box to winning at the highest levels.

Winning Edge: Show Ring Secrets by George Alston applies sports psychology to handling your dog in the ring. The book includes tricks to psych out your competitor as well as a chapter on sportsmanship.

Winning with Purebred Dogs: Success by Design by Al Gossman instructs you on how to buy the right first show dog and how to use a professional handler to your best advantage, in addition to providing "straight facts about judges" among many other topics.

Videos

Handling I (Basic) and *Handling II (Advanced)* by Michael Kemp provides how-to handling advice, starting with novices and working up to more advanced techniques. Each video is 60 minutes long.

Puppy Puzzle: Evaluating Structural Quality by Pat and Bob Hastings provides a comprehensive system for evaluating puppies at 8 weeks of age to help determine which ones will make it in the show ring, which puppies are likely to be good breeding stock, which would excel in physically demanding sports like obedience and agility, and which should be placed as "couch potatoes." This video is 55 minutes long.

Show Dogs by Jeffrey Brucker is a conformation-handling video course for beginner and intermediate handlers. It is two hours long.

JUNIOR HANDLING

Junior handling is a great way for kids to learn about dogs and dog shows. Two popular books written just for juniors are:

Best Junior Handler by Anne and Denise Olejiczak. Written by a junior handler, it includes tips on how to dress, sportsmanship, and the finer points of competition.

FICTION

If you like to read fiction with a backdrop that includes purebred dogs, and sometimes dog shows, check out the following writers:

Carol Lea Benjamin. After a career writing first-class obedience books, Benjamin turned to a life of crime. She has a series of murder mysteries, starring private eye Rachel Alexander and her Pit Bull, Dash.

Laurien Berenson. The theme for Berenson's books is usually murder at the dog show. The series centers around Melanie Travis, a school teacher and amateur sleuth, and her Standard Poodle named Faith (who is working on her show championship). The love interest shows his Standard Poodles in the ring, too.

Emily Carmichael. To date, romance writer Emily Carmichael has only written one doggie romance: *Finding Mr. Right.* It's a very funny tale of a woman who finds herself brought back from life in the body of a rescue Pembroke Welsh Corgi named Miss Piggy.

Susan Conant. Alaskan Malamutes Rowdy and Kimi compete in conformation and obedience, and often literally drag owner and dog writer Holly Winter to the scene of the crime.

Virginia Lanier. Heroine Jo Beth Sidden and her man-hunting Bloodhounds are about as far away from a dog show as you can get, but this writer speaks knowledgeably about the breed. She's lyrical in her description of Bloodhounds trailing through the Okefenokee Swamp, looking for lost souls and bad guys.

ALL-TIME BEST DOG-SHOW WRITER

Albert Payson Terhune. The popular author of *Lad: A Dog* and many other works did much to popularize the Collie in the first half of the century. He also wrote compellingly of purebred dogs and dog shows. An entire generation fell in love with dogs through the words of Terhune. If you can find one of his books at a secondhand store or rare bookstore, buy it and read it. They're magical even today.

Index

Index

Index

Index